THE SHAK... S0-AHH-982

HENRY IV Part 1

THE SHAKESPEARE PLAYS

THE SHAKESPEARE PLAYS

Literary Consultant: John Wilders

Henry IV Part 1

MAYFLOWER BOOKS
NEW YORK

CONTENTS

PREFACE

Cedric Messina

The BBC Television Shakespeare moves into its second year with productions of *Henry IV Part 1*, *Henry IV Part 2*, *Henry V*, *The Tempest*, *Twelfth Night* and *Hamlet*. The plan is to present the thirty-seven plays in groups of six a year for six years, with one odd man out. The productions have now been sold for showing throughout the world, thus fulfilling the public broadcasting ideal behind the series – to make them available to audiences who would have no other access to Shakespeare. Transmissions of the first six plays (*Romeo and Juliet*, *Richard II*, *As You Like It*, *Julius Caesar*, *Measure for Measure* and *Henry VIII*) have already been completed in many countries, notably the USA, Canada and Australia. Japan, Mexico, Hungary, Rumania, Hong Kong, Taiwan, France and many others have bought the plays, but in many cases have not yet finally decided whether they should be dubbed or subtitled. Many of the languages involved have splendid translations of some of the major plays, but only a few have excellent versions of the whole canon.

Thirty-six of the plays were published in the First Folio of 1623, exactly half of which had never been published before. (The thirty-seventh is *Pericles*, *Prince of Tyre*, first published in the Quarto of 1609.) The authoritative text of *Henry IV Part 1* is that of the First Quarto, issued in 1598 under the title '*The History of Henrie the Fourth; With the battell at Shrewsburie, betweene the King and Lord Henry Percy, surnamed Henrie Hotspur of the North. With the humorous conceits of Sir John Falstalffe*'. The production was recorded at the BBC Television Centre at White City, London, in March 1979.

The BBC production of *1 Henry IV* begins with a flashback to *Richard II*, the first pictures on the screen being the murder of Richard in Pomfret Castle, one of the closing episodes of that play. Immediately following this sequence, Bolingbroke, Richard's usurper and now King Henry IV, guilt-ridden by his unlawful possession of the crown reaffirms his determination to make a

7

pilgrimage to Jerusalem, hoping thereby to expiate his guilt. The guilt of the seizing of the crown is as pervasive in Shakespeare's chronicle plays as is the guilt and the curse on the house of Argos in Greek drama, where in the three great plays of Aeschylus' *Oresteia* Atreus and his house carry the burden of the curse for the horrors Atreus perpetrated. In *Richard III*, the eighth and last of the chronicle plays, there is still an echo of Richard II's murder, when Rivers sees Pomfret Castle and evokes Richard's memory.

1 Henry IV, despite its royal trappings, is about a father and his son, and about that son, Prince Hal, and his father-substitute, Sir John Falstaff. In creating Falstaff Shakespeare gave the English stage one of its most durable comic characters, and his relationship with the heir to the throne is one of the most important relationships in the two parts of *Henry IV*. The king can never forgive himself for seizing the crown, and his gloomy court is no place for the high-spirited Hal, who spends all his time with Falstaff and his cronies at the Boar's Head tavern. Around this absurd sun reel satellites like Poins, Bardolph and Mistress Quickly plus their drunken friends. The low-life scenes in Part 1 are some of the most human Shakespeare ever wrote.

The television production of Part 1 brings out very startlingly the great gulf between Henry, his Court and Hal's slightly disapproving brothers. Contrasted with the king is the great corpulent braggadocio Falstaff, and contrasted with Hal is Harry Hotspur, the wild impetuous symbol of the dying chivalry. For a young actor Hotspur is one of the plum parts in the canon of Shakespeare's works, and Tim Pigott-Smith, the Angelo from BBC Television's *Measure for Measure*, underlines the gadfly qualities of the young man whom the king so ardently admires. The king compares him with his own son, a bitter disappointment to him, but his admiration is dimmed when Hotspur and his father join an insurrection against the crown.

One of the many fascinations of seeing the plays in performance is not only seeing Shakespeare's characters progress through the plays, but to watch the actors grow with their parts. In the BBC's *Richard II* the usurper, Bolingbroke, was played by Jon Finch, and here, in the two parts of *Henry IV*, he is transformed into the bitter, pain-racked father who despairs of the future of England under his son. Jon Finch makes a memorable Henry IV, and his constant pain is terrible to see. His son Hal, briefly and disparagingly mentioned in *Richard II*, makes his appearance in the trilogy waking the sleeping and snoring Falstaff, played by Anthony

Quayle, an actor of great distinction and one-time Director of the Shakespeare Memorial Theatre, Stratford-on-Avon, England. Prince Hal is played by David Gwillim, and through the trilogy we watch the young Prince of Wales grow in stature through *2 Henry IV* and into *Henry V*, where we leave him kneeling beside his bride, Princess Katherine of France – a national hero who died at the age of thirty-two. In Hal's first soliloquy 'I know you all' (I ii 88), he explains how he will disguise his firm intention of being a good king when the time comes under a temporary disguise of giddiness and frivolity. The swift cutting from scene to scene in television productions heightens the contrast between Hotspur and Hal. Hotspur with his loving wife and doting father is made to seem more stable than he actually is. When he joins with Mortimer, the legal heir to the throne, and with Owen Glendower the Welsh leader, it is inevitable that he will ultimately end in face-to-face confrontation with the king. One of the play's great scenes is in Glendower's castle when Hotspur and his wife meet with Mortimer and his wife, a Welsh girl who speaks no English, and played before a roaring open fire – a moment of true peace in a play which is constantly being brought back to the troubles of the realm.

The battle with the insurgents is the climax to the play, and the death of Hotspur at the hands of Hal is a savage and bitterly-fought single-handed combat. Hal saves Henry's life, but at a moment of possible reconciliation the king again reopens old wounds by saying that he never thought his son would save him, but allow him to perish and so gain the crown. So the play ends for Henry in renewed pain and misery. But transcending all these domestic and royal brawls, astride a cloud of wit and good humour sits Falstaff enjoying his loves, his friendships and his sack.

It was decided to publish the plays, using the Peter Alexander edition, the same text as used in the production of the plays, and one very widely used in the academic world. But these texts with their theatrical divisions into scenes and acts are supplemented with their television equivalents. In other words we are also publishing the television scripts on which the production was based. There are colour and black and white photographs of the production, a general introduction to the play by Dr John Wilders and an article by Henry Fenwick which includes interviews with the actors, directors, designers and costume designers, giving their reactions to the special problems their contributions encountered in the transfer of the plays to the screen. The volumes include a

9

newly-compiled glossary and a complete cast list of the performers, including the names of the technicians, costume designers and scenic designers responsible for the play.

INTRODUCTION TO
HENRY IV PART 1

John Wilders

Shakespeare devoted four plays – *Richard II, Henry IV Part 1, Henry IV Part 2* and *Henry V* – to the history of England from the time of the rebellion of Henry Bolingbroke against Richard II to the time of Henry V's campaign against the French and his victory at Agincourt. Each play is coherent and intelligible in itself but can also be seen as part of a large-scale historical drama in twenty acts. In these plays Shakespeare does not simply portray the major political events of this period but also shows the reasons why they happened. He explains why Richard was replaced on the throne by Bolingbroke, why, when he became Henry IV, Bolingbroke failed to keep his subjects at peace, how Bolingbroke's son, Prince Hal, prepared himself for his duties as king and why, as Henry V, he created among his people a sense of unity and led them to victory against their traditional enemies, the French. Shakespeare is both a political dramatist and a political analyst.

He wrote *Henry IV Part 1* in about 1597, when he was in his early thirties and had already completed such masterpieces as *Romeo and Juliet, Richard II* and *A Midsummer Night's Dream*. Compared with these earlier plays, *1 Henry IV* is remarkable for the variety and vividness of its characterisation. Practically every character is powerfully and strikingly created: the care-worn King, the enigmatic Prince, the bard-like magician Glendower, the impetuous Hotspur, and Falstaff, the most subtly human personality Shakespeare had yet conceived. There is also a lively collection of minor figures such as Mistress Quickly, Bardolph, Worcester and Lady Percy. Each of them displays his individuality by the uniquely personal language and style of the dialogue Shakespeare has written for him; the speeches of any one character could not be mistaken for those of another.

Here, for example, is Falstaff pondering on the physical evidence of his decline into old age:

> Bardolph, am I not fall'n away vilely since this last action? Do I
> not bate? Do I not dwindle? Why, my skin hangs about me like
> an old lady's loose gown; I am withered like an old apple-john.

Falstaff's homely imagination not only creates a vivid impression
of his own degenerating flesh but conveys his pleasure in language
itself, a pleasure which is, of course, Shakespeare's. A
similarly inventive, delighted use of language can be seen in
Hotspur's explosive speeches, such as his outburst of impatience
against Glendower:

> O, he is as tedious
> As a tired horse, a railing wife;
> Worse than a smoky house; I had rather live
> With cheese and garlic in a windmill, far,
> Than feed on cates and have him talk to me
> In any summer house in Christendom.

Hotspur's tone of voice is totally different from Falstaff's, but both
speeches are expansive, voluble, filled with similes, one growing
apparently spontaneously out of another. Their references,
moreover, are to the intimate details of contemporary domestic life
– an old woman's ample dress, a parlour filled with wood-smoke –
with the result that we are made aware both of the personality of
the man who is speaking and of the small, telling details of the
social life to which he belongs. Shakespeare's history plays have
been called an English epic, and this is true not simply because
they portray the career of a great national hero, Henry V, but
because they convey a brilliant impression of the life of the whole
country.

This variety of character and style is not to be found in the first
of the four plays, *Richard II*, and the difference is probably
deliberate. Shakespeare creates the impression that the deposition
of the hereditary feudal monarch liberated a nation of individual-
ists who found themselves no longer constrained by ancient social
structures but free to assert their personal independence. It is not
only the political revolutionaries, Worcester, Northumberland and
Hotspur, who are rebels. In this play practically everyone is
temperamentally a rebel, including Prince Hal, who appears to
despise his political responsibilities, Falstaff, who abuses his
authority in the war to line his own pockets, and even the King,
who can never forget that he is a usurper. Yet it is the usurper who
has the job of controlling this collection of idiosyncratic, rebellious

individuals in the hope that they may co-operate with him and one another and thereby become a nation. Moreover the usurper, lacking the legal right to govern, has no force to support him other than that of his own personality. The impression he creates on his subjects is all-important.

Henry IV fails to control his people because he suffers the consequences of his seizure of the crown; Prince Hal succeeds partly because he inherits the throne by right of birth and partly because he knows how to win his subjects' loyalty. Whereas the old King provides a link with the past, with the deposition portrayed in *Richard II*, the memory of which haunts him, the young Prince provides a link with the future, with the responsibilities he undertakes in *Henry V*, for which he skilfully prepares himself.

Henry Bolingbroke acquired the throne through the help of the Percy family, Thomas, Earl of Worcester, Henry, Earl of Northumberland, and his son Henry Hotspur. In the early days of the rebellion he took care to ingratiate himself with these men on whom his success depended. But, as *1 Henry IV* opens, he attempts to impose his royal authority over them and thereby provokes their resentment. When, for example, Henry accuses Worcester of disrespect, the latter retorts that the King is indebted to his family for the very power he is now trying to assert:

> Our house, my sovereign liege, little deserves
> The scourge of greatness to be us'd on it –
> And that same greatness too which our own hands
> Have holp to make so portly.

It is their resentment against the man they have themselves placed in authority that provokes the Percys to rebel. They also fear that his sense of dependence on them will prove so embarrassing that he will find a pretext to do away with them:

> For, bear ourselves as even as we can,
> The King will always think him in our debt,
> And think we think ourselves unsatisfied,
> Till he hath found a time to pay us home.

They are determined to overthrow him before he can eradicate them and, consequently, form an alliance with the Welsh and the Scots in an attempt to force their former ally from the throne. Even when, just before the opposing armies meet at Shrewsbury, Henry offers them an amnesty, Worcester persists in his conviction that the King will sooner or later want to dispose of them:

It is not possible, it cannot be,
The King should keep his word in loving us;
He will suspect us still, and find a time
To punish this offence in other faults.

On the basis of this conjecture, Worcester refuses the offered
pardon and proceeds with the attack which costs Hotspur his life.
By one of the ironies of history, of which Shakespeare was much
aware, Henry IV is troubled throughout his reign by the very men
to whom he owed his power.

He is also troubled by his fears for the future. He regards his son
as a contemptible profligate who has cheapened his reputation by
consorting with the common people instead of playing his part in
affairs of state. Hal, he believes, has debased himself with 'vile
participation':

Not an eye
But is aweary of thy common sight,
Save mine, which hath desir'd to see thee more.

For this reason Henry looks forward with dread to his son's
accession to the throne and the derision with which, he believes,
his subjects will treat him. Hal's accession to power is also eagerly
awaited by Falstaff, not with apprehension, but in the hope that
his ally in crime will give him licence to indulge his appetites
without restraint. During their first scene together and in their
charades at the Boar's Head Tavern, Falstaff constantly tests Hal
in order to discover what his own prospects will be when his
companion becomes King.

The impression the audience receives of Hal's conduct does not,
however, correspond with the low opinion held of him by the King
and Falstaff. Although the Prince appears to debase himself by
associating with petty malefactors, he claims that he does so
deliberately as an act of political policy. Unlike Richard II (to
whom his father mistakenly compares him) he is not naturally
dissolute but chooses to appear so in order that, when the need
arises, he may appear miraculously to reform and thereby arouse
the grateful admiration of his people. As he explains in his
soliloquy at the end of the second scene, his association with
Falstaff has been contrived in order to 'falsify men's hopes' so that
his ultimate reformation may 'show more goodly and attract more
eyes'. He intends to gain the loyalty of his subjects by astonishing
them.

In order to rule successfully, the medieval monarch had, ideally, to display two fundamental virtues: justice in time of peace and courage in time of war. Prince Hal demonstrates his possession of the former, the civic virtue, in *2 Henry IV* by placing his trust in the Lord Chief Justice and sending Falstaff to gaol. He reveals the latter, the military virtue, in *Part 1* by the symbolic act of defeating the most distinguished soldier of his age, Henry Hotspur. Hotspur in certain superficial ways resembles Hal. They have the same name, they are about the same age (and Shakespeare altered the historical facts to make their ages similar), both are eager to acquire what they call 'honour', or fame in battle, and, indeed, the King twice compares the two men to Hal's disadvantage. For Hotspur the pursuit of honour is an obsession, an ideal which takes precedence over all others, a reward for which no risk is too great:

> By heaven, methinks it were an easy leap
> To pluck bright honour from the pale-fac'd moon;
> Or dive into the bottom of the deep,
> Where fathom-line could never touch the ground,
> And pluck up drowned honour by the locks;
> So he that doth redeem her thence might wear
> Without corrival all her dignities.

He is a rash, impulsive, spontaneous man, at home only on the battlefield and, like a good many English aristocrats, has as much respect for his horse as for his wife. In his element he is, as everyone agrees, unparalleled, 'the king of honour'. In challenging and defeating Hotspur in single combat, therefore, the Prince is not simply defending his father against a dangerous rebel but giving a public demonstration of his filial loyalty and his superiority in battle over the greatest soldier of his time.

Hotspur is an exciting, even an inspiring figure because of his energetic singlemindedness: he rises with enthusiasm to the challenge of war and welcomes even the desertion of his allies because, without them, he is exposed to greater danger and can thereby win greater honour. But his obsessive preoccupation with war, which is his strength, also makes him appear ridiculous. Off the battlefield, in the domestic surroundings of his home at Warkworth or in the political negotiations with Glendower, he is restless, irritable, tactless and impatient. Hal, though he respects Hotspur, has no wish to copy him. Hal has a larger mind, capable of entering into a wider variety of experiences of which war is only one and which includes his high-spirited association with Falstaff.

Falstaff has as much vitality as Hotspur, and shows a similarly wholehearted dedication to his own way of life and a similar tendency to boast of his prowess. In all other ways the two men are total opposites. Whereas Hotspur is spontaneously truthful, Falstaff has a genius for the inspired lie; whereas Hotspur dedicates himself to honour – and, indeed, dies in the pursuit of it – Falstaff argues that honour is a delusion; whereas Hotspur embraces danger eagerly, Falstaff takes flight after the Gadshill robbery and feigns death in order to survive. He is in many ways repellent: physically grotesque, morally irresponsible, grossly self-indulgent, an ageing rake. He is also one of the most popular and enjoyable characters in the whole of literature. The reason for his popularity is, perhaps, that he represents that part of ourselves which would like to flout moral and social convention, to defy the law and to devote itself without restraint to survival and the gratification of our appetites. He expresses our secret and unattainable desire to remain irresponsible children.

The action of *1 Henry IV* is distributed between three different places, the court, the tavern and the battlefield. Each location has what might be called a presiding character: the King, preoccupied with politics and the instability of the state; Falstaff, dedicated to pleasure and the satisfaction of his appetites; and Hotspur obsessed with revenge on Bolingbroke and the acquisition of martial glory. The only character who moves freely between all three places is the Prince who can be, as the occasion requires, the dutiful son, the willing foil to Falstaff and the responsible and courageous soldier. His adaptability to any society makes him destined to be a popular ruler, capable, when he becomes Henry V, of dealing firmly with the French ambassadors, chatting intimately with the common soldiers and exhorting his troops to victory. Yet this very flexibility of temperament makes him a less forceful, a more elusive and impenetrable personality than anyone else in the play. He responds so readily, so convincingly to everybody that one suspects that he may have no essential personality at all but is a mere reflection of the company he happens to keep. His first scene with Falstaff is particularly revealing – or rather, significantly unrevealing: throughout their conversation he leaves all the initiative to the other man and either shrugs off or evades Falstaff's attempts to discover his intentions. The fact is that the man who was to become the most successful of all English monarchs, the idol of his people, is an enclosed, impenetrable person. His most intimate self, if it exists, remains hidden. To set out deliberately, as a matter of policy, to exploit his association with Falstaff for the sake of his public reputation does not commend him to us. It requires a calculated deception both of his apparent friend and of his future subjects. And, though his policy succeeds to his own advantage and that of the nation, he is guilty of assuming that the means are justified by the end.

Hal is, however, not the only character who tries to make use of others to his own advantage: just as he makes use of Falstaff for political purposes, so Falstaff hopes to profit from Hal on the latter's accession. And if Hal intends to enhance his reputation by defeating Hotspur, then he is merely playing the same game as his rival. In his dying moments Hotspur confesses that he is more deeply wounded by his loss of reputation than by his loss of life:

I better brook the loss of brittle life
Than those proud titles thou hast won of me:
They wound my thoughts worse than thy sword my flesh.

In its assertive vitality, the world of *1 Henry IV* is fiercely competitive: the King makes use of the Percys, Falstaff attempts to profit from Hal, Hotspur competes for honour against the Prince, and Hal is such a master of deception that even his own father is taken in by him. In this competitive world the victory is awarded not to the most morally deserving but to the toughest and the shrewdest. It is Hal who succeeds in the end, and in showing us how he succeeds Shakespeare makes a coldly realistic comment on the nature of politics.

GENEALOGICAL TABLE

This is a simplified table, showing the succession from Edward III to Henry VIII and those characters who are important in *Henry IV*, *Parts 1 & 2* and *Henry V*. The dates refer to lives and not to reigns.

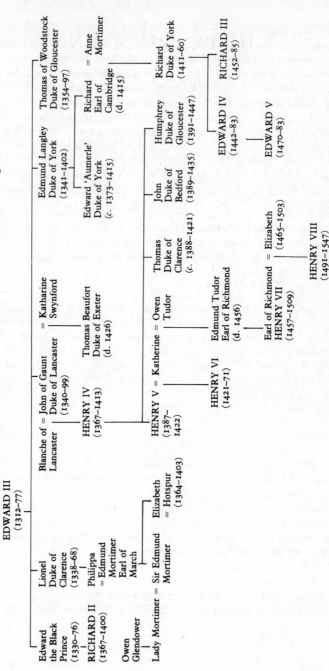

THE PRODUCTION

Henry Fenwick

'The histories, from *Richard II* up to *Henry V*, are, I think,' says producer Cedric Messina, 'the highest achievement of Shakespeare's art. The four plays are simply staggering – I don't think any of the other histories come anywhere near as plays. It seems to me, with a lot of hindsight, that these histories are a sort of Curse of the House of Atreus in English. The curse of the death of Richard permeates *Henry IV* Parts 1 and 2, he's mentioned again in *Henry V*, and he is actually referred to in *Richard III* as well – it goes on and on. The murder of Richard II has tremendous significance in these three pieces. Added to that is the shadow that Richard's legal heir, Mortimer, throws over Part 1; because, apart from Henry's guilt over the death of Richard, he's also terribly suspicious of Mortimer, who as the legal heir of Richard II should have been king of England.'

'Part 1 is a remarkable play – people say that all of life is there, but it's a very specific attitude to life – almost an Oedipal one. Hal deserts his own home because he can't stand the gloom and misery, I think, of Henry IV's court, and finds a kind of substitute father figure in Falstaff; Henry IV bewails the fact that his own son isn't like Harry Hotspur; and it's resolved at the end of Part 1 when, after a couple of very gloomy scenes between father and son, the boy actually saves the king's life.'

'Henry's sickness is not evident at the end of *Richard II*, but at the beginning of *1 Henry IV* he starts off ill. He also starts off in a *very* bad temper when he's told of the usurping rebels and immediately he gives an excuse for not going to Jerusalem in order to expiate his guilt for the murder of Richard. We repeat the scene of that murder at the beginning of the play, and when you actually see it again on the screen it does ram it home.'

'Of course, over both parts of *Henry IV* is the shadow of Falstaff, and Tony Quayle gives a remarkable, marvellous performance. Yet I don't think Shakespeare ever completely explains why Hal is so enamoured of him. There must have been some enormous, intellectual charm. And his good humour and jollity are such a contrast to his father's miseries, which are heaped on everybody around him throughout Part 1, that this explains a lot.'

David Giles directed *Richard II* last year, but at that time was not expecting to continue with the three Henrys. This season he has directed both parts of *Henry IV* and *Henry V*. One of the first problems to face him was that of style: 'I think *Henry IV* Parts 1 and 2 are more realistic than we made *Richard*, because the scenes are so much more private – it all happens in rooms: in the Boar's Head, in Warkworth Castle, and often the scenes are just duologues. I think the biggest problem was finding a style that would also encompass the battle. There is one battle you cannot get past, and that is Shrewsbury in *1 Henry IV*, because there is personal confrontation after personal confrontation. I think we've got through it quite well. What we've used is a very long lens on the camera, so what you see in focus is clear but everything else is blurred. We didn't want to use this just for the battles, so we decided to use it in all the exteriors.'

'David and Tim [David Gwillim as Hal and Tim Pigott-Smith as Hotspur] have the most marvellous fight, really gory, and Tim's death is horrific, extremely nasty.' He chuckles with appreciation. 'They spent hours and hours rehearsing the fight and it does work. One can't do realistic battles because Shakespeare doesn't write realistic battles: you have all this dialogue going on which in reality you just wouldn't have time for – or breath, with those swords and that armour. Anyway, we had a go and I think it works. It's greatly helped, in Shrewsbury, because it keeps being debunked by Falstaff. He's a marvellous safety valve. Just when you are not sure whether to believe this or not he comes on saying, "I don't believe this either and if you were here you'd behave just like me!" Which is very useful.'

The set designer, Don Homfray, expands on the technique of dealing with the battles: 'We used a very narrow lens that focuses a long way – what that does is to reduce the depth of field so that the depth of focus is very shallow. A character is in focus, but perhaps even six inches behind him is out of focus. You get an impressionist view of what is going on. To do that you've got to have space – we were using the big studio and had to clear it: it's a common technique in films today, but you don't normally have the space in television to do it.'

'We thought of the plays as social histories of England, not in fact of the early fifteenth century but of Elizabethan England.

Having said that, we did set it in the period it's historically supposed to be set in, although there are anomalies in the text; but we also tried to get the right sort of texture for the times: making everything very grotty – which it obviously would have been.'

Giles doesn't find the anomalies in the text too worrying. 'When you're dealing with an historical figure like Henry and everybody has a very strong image of him, if you go against that image you're asking for trouble straight away. I think it would be very alienating to put them into Elizabethan dress, even though that is how they were originally performed. Poor Odette [Barrow, the costume designer] of course has to be explicit in showing, for example, a coat of arms which is described wrongly in the play. I think then you've got to be true to the play and not to history because you are doing a play, not a documentary about Henry.'

Odette Barrow says that research for Part I was very difficult for her: 'There were very many aspects to it and I couldn't at first find anyone who had done much work in that period. I found someone too late for Part I. We were also working in a semi-documentary style, which I found very difficult. For instance, when doing the heraldic surcoats for the fighting sequences I had a problem with Hotspur. Historically, when his mother died he incorporated her arms with his. But Shakespeare manages to have her appear in Part 2, *after* Hotspur's death; so we thought, well, we'll have to give him his arms as they were before she died. So as far as history is concerned his arms at the battle of Shrewsbury are therefore inaccurate, but as far as Shakespeare is concerned, they're right. Also it was impossible to be absolutely accurate with the banner carriers – they are actually knights and they should be dressed in armour with their own arms on their surcoats – but I just didn't have enough armour to go around in Part I and simply had to do what I could. I managaed to rectify it in Part 2.'

For the battle scenes she attempted, for the viewers' sakes, to differentiate clearly between the different camps: 'Knights and householders were just beginning to have their own badges at this time and I tried to find badges for them. And I used colour too – soft blues and murky greens for the Welsh; browns and sludgy greens for the English. During the fighting I used surcoats and tried to group soldiers with Douglas's badge or Hotspur's badge, so that the factions are recognisable.'

If there were more problems than usual for the designers, the script editor Alan Shallcross, was luckier. Although the Henry plays are long, Part I is the shortest of the three, and the cuts needed were not too difficult. 'We tended to cut where there was a lot of political talk about what has happened beforehand. There is a constant referring to the theme of the guilt of Richard's death and it was important to keep that, but there are moments where the polemic is endlessly knocked about and that's where we cut.' I ask him about some of the now archaic language in the comic scenes, but, as he points out, 'in the histories the humour lies in character, not in the verbal play, and if the broad outline of the scene is clear it's irrelevant what words like a ferkin or a figo mean.'

David Giles began work on the three plays with a slight, rather unconventional preference for Part 2, but 'fell in love with Part 1 as we worked on it. It's such a beautiful play, wonderfully written. It starts deceptively quietly, then you get into the Boar's Head. The first section of the play, which includes a wonderful confrontation between Hotspur and the King, moves towards the great Boar's Head scene, which runs about eighteen to twenty minutes and which we did as one take. In that scene Falstaff, who represents the King in a way, and the Prince really hammer out in front of us their future relationship. It's so alive and rich and touches so many points of human contact, you think "How is he going to follow this?" And then he writes this magical scene in Wales – in its way just as wonderful – with Glendower, this strange Welsh almost madman, and his daughter, who speaks nothing but Welsh – really the princess in the Enchanted Castle – and there are Hotspur and his wife, and Worcester, who's one of my favourite characters, all trying to make terms. The scene switches in the most extraordinary way and the lady sings and he's capped it! He's moved on but not let you down at all. Then you move on to a painful duologue between the King and the Prince and you go on with the play. Although he's written this huge set piece he isn't floored by it! Because of the strong Hotspur plot you get a wonderful juxtaposition of scenes with Falstaff and Prince Hal. Hotspur is the real image of the golden boy, stupid as they come in some ways, but wonderfully noble and honourable in the true sense of the word. And in two short scenes with Hotspur and Lady Percy, Shakespeare writes one of the most superb married relationships in all of his plays.'

'I found out, with great interest, that in fact Hal was one of the hostages Bolingbroke gave to Richard when Richard went to Ireland. Richard treated Hal very well when he could indeed have been extremely nasty; so when Richard's murder comes and Hal's father takes over the throne, to some extent it explains Hal's reaction against his father. One feels a need to explain that extreme reaction against Henry and the taking of Falstaff as a surrogate father figure, who is the exact opposite of the King. Communication between Henry IV and his son are absolutely terrible: the scenes they have together are always extremely painful and always turn out in a different way from what one might expect. For instance, the big scene where Henry has Hal on the carpet should really finish up with Hal crying and Henry being the headmaster, but it ends up completely the other way round: Henry becomes so involved with his guilt for the death of Richard it's he who's crying and Hal who is steadying him. Then all the time Hal is being compared to Hotspur and he keeps saying, "Wait until the real confrontation comes, then you'll see who the real strong man is." There is not room for both of them in the kingdom and it is Hal who kills Hotspur. As the sword goes in, the scales drop from Hotspur's eyes – he sees that all the honour he has accrued will now go to Hal, a very bitter death. But one also feels that in the last speech Hal meets someone who is nearly his equal and given other circumstances they could have been great friends.'

'It's very difficult to work out a logical line for Hotspur's behaviour,' says Tim Pigott-Smith. The part is almost diametrically opposite to his role in last season's *Measure for Measure*, when he played Angelo, corrupt and clever. 'One of the key things about Hotspur is that he's an irrational man, emotionally violent, goes off at a tangent, acts off the top of his head, so I had to act it that way – off the top of my head. Everybody says what a great bloke he is but we see him at his most childish. He's very indiscreet, he lets the plot out, which is exactly what he's been warned not to do, his wife has to treat him like a child, he behaves appallingly badly to Glendower. It's only at the end he achieves rational status. He does wind up being genuinely heroic, and the irony is that he then becomes the butt of Falstaff's "What is honour?" speech. He ends up slung head down across Falstaff's back – the most humiliating image we could find. We worked very hard on the fights, trying to take them away from the noble image. There's quite a bit of rolling around, nothing noble about it – we just hack away.'

Jon Finch did not know, when he played Bolingbroke in *Richard II* last year, that he would be asked this year to continue the portrait as *Henry IV*. He was very pleased to do so, though, since he has been anxious for a long time to do more Shakespeare. An actor who has worked primarily in television and films, he has little Shakespearian theatre background. Playing Macbeth in Roman Polanski's film was in fact the first Shakespeare he had ever done, so he was understandably insecure when he came to work alongside Sir John Gielgud and Derek Jacobi last year. 'I was very, very nervous, especially being with Gielgud, and he actually said to me after the read through: "Where did you learn to speak verse?" and I said "As a matter of fact, nowhere," because I never went to drama school, and he said "You speak verse wonderfully". He actually said that to me! I couldn't believe it. It immediately made me feel better and I was relaxed during the rest of the rehearsals.'

Giles was impressed by the way Finch developed the character through the three plays: 'I've never seen a Henry IV like it; it's so edgy and dangerous. I remember Tim [Pigott-Smith] saying in the counsel scene in *1 Henry IV* how marvellous it was to play "because of that paranoiac at the other end of the table".'

Finch is a very physical actor, and it was in the ageing and sickening of Henry that he found most of the challenge and most of the difficulty. It is a strange part – important but less showy than the other principals. 'Someone told me a story,' he laughs when I ask him about this. 'Apparently when one well-known actor was playing the part at Stratford, the energies of the production were very involved with Hal and Hotspur and Falstaff and he said: "The title of this play is in fact Henry IV, Part 1, not Hotspur, not Falstaff and it's not Henry V yet!", and I thought, yes, well, I'll have to cope with that!'

David Gwillim, who plays Hal, knows the play well – he has seen many productions, played Pistol at school and Fluellen in regional theatre, but has never played Hal before. Knowing the play, he says, 'cuts both ways: if you have a clear vision of the play that's fine, but on the other hand you can have a *set* vision of the play as opposed to any sense of exploration. But the time is so restricted with television that it's good to have a clear view. The plays aren't a straightforward dramatic progression – they cover many of the same areas and topics: Shakespeare tends to cover all the angles in each play, so there are speeches in *Henry V* which echo *Henry IV*. In his very first scene Hal sets out what he intends to do, what he's aiming for: so it's not as though he's surprised that he rejects Falstaff when he does in Part 2. The plays are single statements – they aren't like a classic serial on BBC2, there's none of that element at all really; but they do lead into one another. And each play makes different demands: Part 1 is very much entwined with Falstaff – in some ways it's more of a comedy part, though you can't think in those terms on television: there is a lot of comedy but Falstaff becomes much more a living, breathing person on television. On stage there's the big chap with a fat belly, but on television the camera goes right in and you see those frightened eyes! It's ludicrous, it's amusing, but . . .'

Anthony Quayle is playing Falstaff for the third time, returning to the part after a lapse of twenty-five years. The first time was in a now fabled production with Richard Burton as Hal, when Quayle was director at Stratford on Avon. 'When I played it in 1951 I was in my thirties,' he remembers, 'and I was terribly worried that I was too – well, I was never slight, but I wasn't a great fat man and I was much too young, and I had to groan and pad and puff myself out just to convince people I was in my sixties. Nobody knows how old Falstaff is but I'm sure he's well over sixty. I was sixty-five when I did it this time and I didn't have to be so preoccupied convincing people I'm not just a little boy pretending to be an old man. I could grow my own white whiskers and I thought "Well, this time Falstaff is going to look like me".'

The greatest problem in playing the part for television, he found, was in judging the scale of the performance. 'If you're playing Falstaff in the theatre he is a titanic character – in Part 1 he dominates: in Part 2 there's a long period where he goes completely quiet, but never in Part 1. He's ebullient, he's on top of everything; he's a very, very big character. In the theatre the very fact that you have to project to reach the back of the auditorium helps you to be big but if you're doing it for a tiny screen you've an enormous problem: you don't know how big to make him, how broad is his behaviour, because it could just seem like a grotesque piece of overacting. Equally, if you misgauge it you'll make it so small that the whole of the man's scale and size and breadth is just lost. You've got to hit it like a moonshot, and I found it impossible to gauge. In a film you would do several tests and then look at it and say "I see, that's awful, that's overboard, that's under" – you'd find out. With television you never can see yourself. I was totally in David Giles' sensitive and alert hands. But when you come to the three fraught days in the studio you know the poor guy's got to bring it in on schedule and if it's gross he'll tell you, but you're only part of a machine he's got to keep driving. He can't stop. He did in fact say "We'll do that scene again because it isn't quite as good as you can make it", but time is very limited.'

'Parts 1 and 2 are not one play but one is a codicil to the other:

they're not as tightly connected as, say, Durrell's *Alexandria Quartet*, but they are awfully linked. When you look at Part I Falstaff is a merry old lord of misrule, a misleader of the Prince but buoyant, gay, merry, and glorious, glorious company. I think Shakespeare sets up two extreme characters: Hotspur and Falstaff – the first who says "honour, honour" to an exaggerated extent, and the other who is the debunker of any moral standard by which anybody lives. They're presented, it seems to me, absolutely in antithesis – though this makes it sound more calculated than I'm sure it was. Somewhere between the two extremes is Hal. When you do Part I on its own and you have an Olivier playing Hotspur you think "But this is the hero of the play, he's wonderful, Hotspur; I can't bear it if this little prig, Hal, defeats him." Actually I believe Hotspur and Falstaff are a corrective to each other and alongside Hotspur's excessive obsession with honour you see Falstaff's total debunking of it. I don't know about you, but I've lived my life with an endless number of unsolved moral questions: there's a part of me and you and all the audience that says "Falstaff's right", but yet in the last resort if we lived like that we would never have fought Hitler.'

'I would argue that it's the greatest part that Shakespeare ever wrote – possibly Hamlet and Falstaff are the two greatest parts. Falstaff is a force in life, walking the streets here. He's inside all of us. He's also one of the most intelligent characters Shakespeare ever wrote, and you can't play a man as intelligent as that, who is also held up to a great deal of obloquy and scorn, and not know that you are to be ashamed of yourself somehow. I don't believe Falstaff can mock and deride the mores of the world without also having an appreciation of them. Somewhere in your heart there's a desperate sadness: somewhere through all this flesh and "Ha, ha, ha" he's not a roguey-poguey Father Christmas: he knows the grief of the loss of youth, the loss of potency. Yet even when he knows he's finished, Shakespeare never lets him give in. He's a paradox: he scorns honour, he behaves in a terrible way, yet he bears himself honourably. His last gesture is to say: "Come and have dinner with me," yet he has nothing to pay the bill! Where's he going to get the money from? He's a winner and a loser at the same time. He knows how a man should live but he goes his own way. To my mind you should be thinking; "He's adorable but he's ghastly." He's a little boy who's being evil and knows it and knows he'll be punished for it. A miracle of a character. I suppose finally I think he's Shakespeare's greatest character because of the humour and the self-criticism, the wit and wisdom to understand, and the humour to castigate himself as well as the rest of the world: he is the character with the greatest understanding of the agony of living.'

THE BBC TV CAST AND PRODUCTION TEAM

The cast for the BBC television production was as follows:

KING HENRY IV	Jon Finch
HENRY, PRINCE OF WALES	David Gwillim
JOHN OF LANCASTER	Rob Edwards
EARL OF WESTMORELAND	David Buck
SIR WALTER BLUNT	Robert Brown
THOMAS PERCY, EARL OF WORCESTER	Clive Swift
HENRY PERCY, EARL OF NORTHUMBERLAND	Bruce Purchase
HENRY PERCY, HOTSPUR	Tim Pigott-Smith
EDMUND MORTIMER, EARL OF MARCH	Robert Morris
EARL OF DOUGLAS	John Cairney
SCROOP, ARCHBISHOP OF YORK	David Neal
SIR MICHAEL	Norman Rutherford
OWEN GLENDOWER	Richard Owens
SIR RICHARD VERNON	Terence Wilton
SIR JOHN FALSTAFF	Anthony Quayle
POINS	Jack Galloway
BARDOLPH	Gordon Gostelow
PETO	Steven Beard
LADY PERCY	Michele Dotrice
LADY MORTIMER	Sharon Morgan
MISTRESS QUICKLY	Brenda Bruce
FIRST CARRIER	Mike Lewin
SECOND CARRIER	David Bailie
CHAMBERLAIN	Douglas Milvain
SHERIFF	Neville Barber
SERVANT TO HOTSPUR	George Winter
FIRST MESSENGER	Michael Heath

SECOND MESSENGER	Malcolm Hughes
FIGHT ARRANGER	Terry Walsh
PRODUCTION ASSISTANT	Jenny Macarthur
DIRECTOR'S ASSISTANT	Beryl Watts
PRODUCTION UNIT MANAGER	Fraser Lowden
MUSIC ADVISER	David Lloyd-Jones
LITERARY CONSULTANT	John Wilders
MAKE-UP ARTIST	Elizabeth Moss
COSTUME DESIGNER	Odette Barrow
SOUND	Colin Dixon
LIGHTING	Dennis Channon
DESIGNER	Don Homfray
SCRIPT EDITOR	Alan Shallcross
PRODUCER	Cedric Messina
DIRECTOR	David Giles

The production was recorded between 7 and 12 March 1979.

THE TEXT

In order to help readers who might wish to use this text to follow the play on the screen the scene divisions and locations used in the television production and any cuts and rearrangements made are shown in the right-hand margins. The principles governing these annotations are as follows:

1. Where a new location (change of set) is used by the TV production this is shown as a new scene. The scenes are numbered consecutively, and each one is identified as exterior or interior, located by a brief description of the set of the location, and placed in its 'time' setting (e.g. Day, Night, Dawn). These procedures are those used in BBC Television camera scripts.

2. Where the original stage direction shows the entry of a character at the beginning of a scene, this has not been deleted (unless it causes confusion). This is in order to demonstrate which characters are in the scene, since in most cases the TV scene begins with the characters 'discovered' on the set.

3. Where the start of a TV scene does not coincide with the start of a scene in the printed text, the characters in that scene have been listed, *unless* the start of the scene coincides with a stage direction which indicates the entrance of all those characters.

4. Where the text has been cut in the TV production, the cuts are marked by vertical rules and by a note in the margin. If complete lines are cut these are shown as, e.g., Lines 27–38 omitted. If part of a line only is cut, or in cases of doubt (e.g. in prose passages), the first and last words of the cut are also given.

5. Occasionally, and only when it is thought necessary for comprehension of the action, a note of a character's moves has been inserted in the margin.

6. Where the action moves from one part of a set to another, no attempt has been made to show this as a succession of scenes.

ALAN SHALLCROSS

1 HENRY IV

DRAMATIS PERSONÆ

KING HENRY THE FOURTH.
HENRY, PRINCE OF WALES,
PRINCE JOHN OF LANCASTER, } *sons of Henry IV.*

EARL OF WESTMORELAND,
SIR WALTER BLUNT, } *friends of the King.*

THOMAS PERCY, EARL OF WORCESTER.
HENRY PERCY, EARL OF NORTHUMBERLAND.
HENRY PERCY, *surnamed* HOTSPUR, *his son.*
EDMUND MORTIMER, EARL OF MARCH.
ARCHIBALD, EARL OF DOUGLAS.
SCROOP, ARCHBISHOP OF YORK.
SIR MICHAEL, *friend of the Archbishop.*

OWEN GLENDOWER.
SIR RICHARD VERNON.
SIR JOHN FALSTAFF,
POINS,
BARDOLPH,
PETO,
*GADSHILL, } *irregular humorists.*

LADY PERCY, *wife of Hotspur and sister of Mortimer.*
LADY MORTIMER, *wife of Mortimer and daughter of Glendower.*
HOSTESS QUICKLY, *of the Boar's Head, Eastcheap.*
Lords, Officers, Attendants, Sheriff, Vintner, Chamberlain, Drawers, Carriers, Travellers.

*In the television production the part of Gadshill is omitted.

Before the play opens we see, in flashback from the production of *Richard II*, the death of King Richard, from whom King Henry IV seized the Crown of England.

SCENE 1
Interior, London.
The Royal Palace.
Morning
The KING is praying.

SCENE 2
Interior. London.
The Royal Palace.
Morning.

THE SCENE: *England and Wales.*

ACT ONE

SCENE I. *London. The palace.*

Enter the KING, LORD JOHN OF LANCASTER, EARL OF WESTMORELAND, SIR WALTER BLUNT, *and* Others.

KING. So shaken as we are, so wan with care,
Find we a time for frighted peace to pant
And breathe short-winded accents of new broils
To be commenc'd in strands afar remote.
No more the thirsty entrance of this soil   5
Shall daub her lips with her own children's blood;
No more shall trenching war channel her fields,
Nor bruise her flow'rets with the armed hoofs
Of hostile paces.   Those opposed eyes
Which, like the meteors of a troubled heaven,   10
All of one nature, of one substance bred,
Did lately meet in the intestine shock
And furious close of civil butchery,
Shall now in mutual well-beseeming ranks
March all one way, and be no more oppos'd   15
Against acquaintance, kindred, and allies.
The edge of war, like an ill-sheathed knife,

31

No more shall cut his master.   Therefore, friends,
As far as to the sepulchre of Christ—
Whose soldier now, under whose blessed cross   20
We are impressed and engag'd to fight—
Forthwith a power of English shall we levy,
Whose arms were moulded in their mothers' womb
To chase these pagans in those holy fields
Over whose acres walk'd those blessed feet   25
Which fourteen hundred years ago were nail'd
For our advantage on the bitter cross.
But this our purpose now is twelvemonth old,
And bootless 'tis to tell you we will go ;
Therefore we meet not now.   Then let me hear   30
Of you, my gentle cousin Westmoreland,
What yesternight our Council did decree
In forwarding this dear expedience.
WEST. My liege, this haste was hot in question
And many limits of the charge set down   35
But yesternight, when all athwart there came
A post from Wales loaden with heavy news ;
Whose worst was that the noble Mortimer,
Leading the men of Herefordshire to fight
Against the irregular and wild Glendower,   40
Was by the rude hands of that Welshman taken,
A thousand of his people butchered ;
Upon whose dead corpse there was such misuse,
Such beastly shameless transformation,
By those Welshwomen done, as may not be   45
Without much shame re-told or spoken of.
KING. It seems then that the tidings of this broil
Brake off our business for the Holy Land.
WEST. This match'd with other did, my gracious Lord ;
For more uneven and unwelcome news   50
Came from the north, and thus it did import :
On Holy-rood day, the gallant Hotspur there,
Young Harry Percy, and brave Archibald,
That ever-valiant and approved Scot,
At Holmedon met,   55
Where they did spend a sad and bloody hour ;
As by discharge of their artillery
And shape of likelihood the news was told ;
For he that brought them, in the very heat
And pride of their contention did take horse,   60
Uncertain of the issue any way.
KING. Here is a dear, a true industrious friend,
Sir Walter Blunt, new lighted from his horse,
Stain'd with the variation of each soil
Betwixt that Holmedon and this seat of ours ;   65
And he hath brought us smooth and welcome news.
The Earl of Douglas is discomfited :
Ten thousand bold Scots, two and twenty knights,
Balk'd in their own blood, did Sir Walter see
On Holmedon's plains ; of prisoners, Hotspur took   70
Mordake, Earl of Fife and eldest son

To beaten Douglas ; and the Earl of Athol,
Of Murray, Angus, and Menteith.
And is not this an honourable spoil ?
A gallant prize ?   Ha, cousin, is it not ?   75
WEST. In faith,
  It is a conquest for a prince to boast of.
KING. Yea, there thou mak'st me sad and mak'st me sin
  In envy that my Lord Northumberland
  Should be the father to so blest a son—   80
  A son who is the theme of honour's tongue ;
  Amongst a grove, the very straightest plant ;
  Who is sweet Fortune's minion and her pride ;
  Whilst I, by looking on the praise of him,
  See riot and dishonour stain the brow   85
  Of my young Harry.   O that it could be prov'd
  That some night-tripping fairy had exchang'd
  In cradle-clothes our children where they lay,
  And call'd mine Percy, his Plantagenet !
  Then would I have his Harry, and he mine.   90
  But let him from my thoughts.   What think you, coz,
  Of this young Percy's pride ?   The prisoners
  Which he in this adventure hath surpris'd
  To his own use he keeps ; and sends me word,
  I shall have none but Mordake Earl of Fife.   95
WEST. This is his uncle's teaching, this is Worcester,
  Malevolent to you in all aspects ;
  Which makes him prune himself, and bristle up
  The crest of youth against your dignity.
KING. But I have sent for him to answer this ;   100
  And for this cause awhile we must neglect
  Our holy purpose to Jerusalem.
  Cousin, on Wednesday next our council we
  Will hold at Windsor—so inform the lords ;
  But come yourself with speed to us again,   105
  For more is to be said and to be done
  Than out of anger can be uttered.
WEST. I will, my liege.   [*Exeunt.*

SCENE II. *London.   The* PRINCE'S *lodging.*

Enter the PRINCE OF WALES *and* SIR JOHN FALSTAFF.

FAL. Now, Hal, what time of day is it, lad ?
PRINCE. Thou art so fat-witted with drinking of old sack, and un-
  buttoning thee after supper, and sleeping upon benches after
  noon, that thou hast forgotten to demand that truly which thou
  wouldest truly know.   What a devil hast thou to do with the
  time of the day ?   Unless hours were cups of sack, and minutes
  capons, and clocks the tongues of bawds, and dials the signs of
  leaping-houses, and the blessed sun himself a fair hot wench in
  flame-coloured taffeta, I see no reason why thou shouldst be so
  superfluous to demand the time of the day.   11
FAL. Indeed, you come near me now, Hal ; for we that take purses
  go by the moon and the seven stars, and not by Phœbus, he
  ' that wand'ring knight so fair'.   And, I prithee, sweet wag, when

SCENE 3
Interior. Eastcheap.
A small room in the
Boar's Head Tavern.
Morning.
PRINCE OF WALES,
SIR JOHN FALSTAFF.

El Donzel del Febo, Knight of the Sun (Phoebus)

thou art a king, as, God save thy Grace—Majesty, I should say; for grace thou wilt have none—

PRINCE. What, none?

FAL. No, by my troth; not so much as will serve to be prologue to an egg and butter.   20

PRINCE. Well, how then? Come, roundly, roundly.

FAL. Marry, then, sweet wag, when thou art king, let not us that are squires of the night's body be called thieves of the day's beauty; let us be Diana's foresters, gentlemen of the shade, minions of the moon; and let men say we be men of good government, being governed, as the sea is, by our noble and chaste mistress the moon, under whose countenance we steal.

'and let men . . . we steal' omitted.

PRINCE. Thou sayest well, and it holds well too; for the fortune of us that are the moon's men doth ebb and flow like the sea, being governed, as the sea is, by the moon. As, for proof, now: a purse of gold most resolutely snatch'd on Monday night, and most dissolutely spent on Tuesday morning; got with swearing 'Lay by' and spent with crying 'Bring in'; now in as low an ebb as the foot of the ladder, and by and by in as high a flow as the ridge of the gallows.

'got with swearing . . . Bring in' omitted.

FAL. By the Lord, thou say'st true, lad. And is not my hostess of the tavern a most sweet wench?   39

PRINCE. As the honey of Hybla, my old lad of the castle. And is not a buff jerkin a most sweet robe of durance?

'And is not my hostess . . . heir apparent – but' omitted.

FAL. How now, how now, mad wag! What, in thy quips and thy quiddities? What a plague have I to do with a buff jerkin?   45

PRINCE. Why, what a pox have I to do with my hostess of the tavern?

FAL. Well, thou hast call'd her to a reckoning many a time and oft.

PRINCE. Did I ever call for thee to pay thy part?   50

FAL. No; I'll give thee thy due, thou hast paid all there.

PRINCE. Yea, and elsewhere, so far as my coin would stretch; and where it would not, I have used my credit.   54

FAL. Yea, and so us'd it that, were it not here apparent that thou art heir apparent—but, I prithee, sweet wag, shall there be gallows standing in England when thou art king, and resolution thus fubb'd as it is with the rusty curb of old father antic the law? Do not thou, when thou art king, hang a thief.   60

PRINCE. No; thou shalt.

FAL. Shall I? O rare! By the Lord, I'll be a brave judge!

PRINCE. Thou judgest false already: I mean thou shalt have the hanging of the thieves, and so become a rare hangman.   66

FAL. Well, Hal, well; and in some sort it jumps with my humour as well as waiting in the court, I can tell you.

PRINCE. For obtaining of suits?

FAL. Yea, for obtaining of suits, whereof the hangman hath no lean wardrobe. 'Sblood, I am as melancholy as a gib cat or a lugg'd bear.   72

PRINCE. Or an old lion, or a lover's lute.

FAL. Yea, or the drone of a Lincolnshire bagpipe.

PRINCE. What sayest thou to a <u>hare</u>, or the melancholy of Moor Ditch?   76

Eating the flesh of a hare was supposed to generate melancholy.

FAL. Thou hast the most unsavoury similes, and art indeed the most comparative, rascalliest, sweet young prince. But, Hal, I prithee,

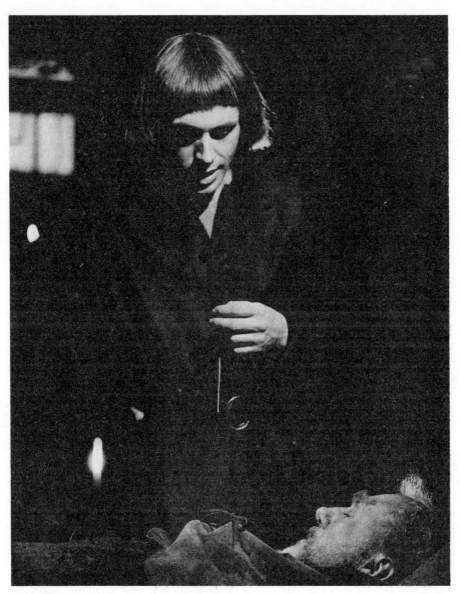

David Gwillim as Prince Hal with Anthony Quayle as Falstaff

trouble me no more with vanity. I would to God thou and I knew where a commodity of good names were to be bought. An old lord of the Council rated me the other day in the street about you, sir, but I mark'd him not; and yet he talk'd very wisely, but I regarded him not; and yet he talk'd wisely, and in the street too.   85

PRINCE. Thou didst well; <u>for wisdom cries out in the streets, and no man regards it.</u>   *Proverbs I:20*

FAL. O, thou hast damnable iteration, and art indeed able to corrupt a saint. Thou hast done much harm upon me, Hal—God forgive thee for it! Before I knew thee, Hal, I knew nothing; and now am I, if a man should speak truly, little better than one of the wicked. I must give over this life, and I will give it over. By the Lord, an I do not I am a villain! I'll be damn'd for never a king's son in Christendom.   95

PRINCE. Where shall we take a purse to-morrow, Jack?

FAL. Zounds, where thou wilt, lad: I'll make one. An I do not, call me villain and baffle me.

PRINCE. I see a good amendment of life in thee—from praying to purse-taking.   100

FAL. Why, Hal, 'tis my vocation, Hal; 'tis no sin for a man to labour in his vocation.   There is a sound of whistling.

Enter POINS. | Omitted.

Poins!—Now shall we know if Gadshill have set a match. O, if men were to be saved by merit, what hole in hell were hot enough for him? This is the most omnipotent villain that ever cried 'Stand' to a true man.   106   'This is the most . . . true man' omitted. POINS enters at this point.

PRINCE. Good morrow, Ned.

POINS. Good morrow, sweet Hal. What says Monsieur Remorse? What says Sir John Sack and Sugar? Jack, how agrees the devil and thee about thy soul, that thou soldest him on Good Friday last for a cup of Madeira and a cold capon's leg?   112

PRINCE. Sir John stands to his word—the devil shall have his bargain; for he was never yet a breaker of proverbs; he will give the devil his due.   'the devil . . . of proverbs' omitted.

POINS. Then art thou damn'd for keeping thy word with the devil.

PRINCE. Else he had been damn'd for cozening the devil.   119

POINS. But, my lads, my lads, to-morrow morning, by four o'clock early, at Gadshill! There are pilgrims going to Canterbury with rich offerings, and traders riding to London with fat purses. I have vizards for you all; you have horses for yourselves. Gadshill lies to-night in Rochester; I have bespoke supper to-morrow night in Eastcheap. We may do it as secure as sleep. If you will go, I will stuff your purses full of crowns; if you will not, tarry at home and be hang'd.   For 'Gadshill' read 'Peto'.

FAL. Hear ye, Yedward: if I tarry at home and go not, I'll hang you for going.   130

POINS. You will, chops?

FAL. Hal, wilt thou make one?

PRINCE. Who?—I rob, I a thief? Not I, by my faith.

FAL. There's neither honesty, manhood, nor good fellowship in thee, nor thou cam'st not of the blood royal, if thou darest not stand for ten shillings.

PRINCE. Well then, once in my days I'll be a madcap.
FAL. Why, that's well said.
PRINCE. Well, come what will, I'll tarry at home.
FAL. By the lord, I'll be a traitor then, when thou art king.   141
PRINCE. I care not.
POINS. Sir John, I prithee, leave the Prince and me alone : I will
  lay him down such reasons for this adventure that he shall go.
FAL. Well, God give thee the spirit of persuasion, and him the ears
  of profiting, that what thou speakest may move, and what he
  hears may be believed ; that the true prince may, for recreation
  sake, prove a false thief ; for the poor abuses of the time want
  countenance.   Farewell ; you shall find me in Eastcheap.   151
PRINCE. Farewell, thou latter spring ! Farewell, All-hallown summer !
                                                        [Exit FALSTAFF.
POINS. Now, my good sweet honey lord, ride with us to-morrow.
  I have a jest to execute that I cannot manage alone.   Falstaff,
  Bardolph, Peto, and Gadshill, shall rob those men that we have
  already waylaid ; yourself and I will not be there ; and when
  they have the booty, if you and I do not rob them, cut this head
  off from my shoulders.   160
PRINCE. How shall we part with them in setting forth ?
POINS. Why, we will set forth before or after them, and appoint
  them a place of meeting, wherein it is at our pleasure to fail ;
  and then will they adventure upon the exploit themselves ; which
  they shall have no sooner achieved but we'll set upon them. 167
PRINCE. Yea, but 'tis like that they will know us by our horses, by
  our habits, and by every other appointment, to be ourselves.
POINS. Tut ! our horses they shall not see—I'll tie them in the wood ;
  our vizards we will change after we leave them ; and, sirrah, I
  have cases of buckram for the nonce, to immask our noted out-
  ward garments.   174
PRINCE. Yea, but I doubt they will be too hard for us.
POINS. Well, for two of them, I know them to be as true-bred cowards
  as ever turn'd back ; and for the third, if he fight longer than
  he sees reason, I'll forswear arms.   The virtue of this jest will
  be the incomprehensible lies that this same fat rogue will tell us
  when we meet at supper : how thirty, at least, he fought with ;
  what wards, what blows, what extremities he endured ; and in
  the reproof of this lives the jest.   183
PRINCE. Well, I'll go with thee.   Provide us all things necessary,
  and meet me to-morrow night in Eastcheap ; there I'll sup.
  Farewell.
POINS. Farewell, my lord.   [Exit POINS.
PRINCE. I know you all, and will awhile uphold
  The unyok'd humour of your idleness ;
  Yet herein will I imitate the sun,   190
  Who doth permit the base contagious clouds
  To smother up his beauty from the world,
  That, when he please again to be himself,
  Being wanted, he may be more wond'red at
  By breaking through the foul and ugly mists   195
  Of vapours that did seem to strangle him.
  If all the year were playing holidays,
  To sport would be as tedious as to work ;

Lines 138–142
omitted.

'and Gadshill'
omitted.

'and appoint them
. . . upon them'
omitted.

But when they seldom come, they wish'd-for come,
And nothing pleaseth but rare accidents.   200
So, when this loose behaviour I throw off
And pay the debt I never promised,
By how much better than my word I am,
By so much shall I falsify men's hopes ;
And, like bright metal on a sullen ground,   205
My reformation, glitt'ring o'er my fault,
Shall show more goodly and attract more eyes
Than that which hath no foil to set it off.
I'll so offend to make offence a skill,
Redeeming time when men think least I will.   [*Exit.*

SCENE III.   *London.   The palace.*

Enter the KING, NORTHUMBERLAND, WORCESTER, HOTSPUR, SIR WALTER
BLUNT, *with* Others.

KING. My blood hath been too cold and temperate,
Unapt to stir at these indignities,
And you have found me ; for accordingly
You tread upon my patience.   But be sure
I will from henceforth rather be myself,   5
Mighty and to be fear'd, than my condition,
Which hath been smooth as oil, soft as young down,
And therefore lost that title of respect
Which the proud soul ne'er pays but to the proud.
WOR. Our house, my sovereign liege, little deserves   10
The scourge of greatness to be us'd on it—
And that same greatness too which our own hands
Have holp to make so portly.
NORTH. My lord—
KING. Worcester, get thee gone ; for I do see   15
Danger and disobedience in thine eye.
O, sir, your presence is too bold and peremptory,
And majesty might never yet endure
The moody frontier of a servant brow.
You have good leave to leave us ; when we need   20
Your use and counsel, we shall send for you.   [*Exit* WORCESTER,
You were about to speak.
NORTH.   Yea, my good lord.
Those prisoners in your Highness' name demanded,
Which Harry Percy here at Holmedon took,
Were, as he says, not with such strength denied   25
As is delivered to your Majesty.
Either envy, therefore, or misprision
Is guilty of this fault, and not my son.
HOT. My liege, I did deny no prisoners.
But I remember when the fight was done,   30
When I was dry with rage and extreme toil,
Breathless and faint, leaning upon my sword,
Came there a certain lord, neat, and trimly dress'd,
Fresh as a bridegroom, and his chin new reap'd
Show'd like a stubble-land at harvest-home.   35
He was perfumed like a milliner,

SCENE 4
*Interior. Windsor
Castle. A Council
Chamber. Afternoon.*

38

King Henry IV (Jon Finch) in Council

And 'twixt his finger and his thumb he held
A pouncet-box, which ever and anon
He gave his nose and took't away again ;
Who therewith angry, when it next came there,   40
Took it in snuff—and still he smil'd and talk'd—
And as the soldiers bore dead bodies by,
He call'd them untaught knaves, unmannerly,
To bring a slovenly unhandsome corse
Betwixt the wind and his nobility.   45
With many holiday and lady terms
He questioned me : amongst the rest, demanded
My prisoners in your Majesty's behalf.
I then, all smarting with my wounds being cold,
To be so pest'red with a popinjay,   50
Out of my grief and my impatience
Answer'd neglectingly I know not what—
He should, or he should not—for he made me mad
To see him shine so brisk, and smell so sweet,
And talk so like a waiting-gentlewoman   55
Of guns, and drums, and wounds—God save the mark !—
And telling me the sovereignest thing on earth
Was parmaceti for an inward bruise ;
And that it was great pity, so it was,
This villainous saltpetre should be digg'd   60
Out of the bowels of the harmless earth,
Which many a good tall fellow had destroy'd
So cowardly ; and but for these vile guns
He would himself have been a soldier.
This bald unjointed chat of his, my lord,   65
I answered indirectly, as I said ;
And I beseech you, let not his report
Come current for an accusation
Betwixt my love and your high Majesty.
BLUNT. The circumstance considered, good my lord,   70
Whate'er Lord Harry Percy then had said
To such a person, and in such a place,
At such a time, with all the rest re-told,
May reasonably die, and never rise
To do him wrong, or any way impeach   75
What then he said, so he unsay it now.
KING. Why, yet he doth deny his prisoners,
But with proviso and exception—
That we at our own charge shall ransom straight
His brother-in-law, the foolish Mortimer ;   80
Who, on my soul, hath wilfully betray'd
The lives of those that he did lead to fight
Against that great magician, damn'd Glendower,
Whose daughter, as we hear, that Earl of March   **For 'Earl of March'**
Hath lately married.   Shall our coffers, then,   85 **read 'Mortimer'.**
Be emptied to redeem a traitor home ?
Shall we buy treason, and indent with fears,
When they have lost and forfeited themselves ?
No, on the barren mountains let him starve ;
For I shall never hold that man my friend   90

Whose tongue shall ask me for one penny cost
To ransom home revolted Mortimer.
HOT. Revolted Mortimer!
He never did fall off, my sovereign liege,
But by the chance of war; to prove that true,   95
Needs no more but one tongue for all those wounds,
Those mouthed wounds, which valiantly he took
When on the gentle Severn's sedgy bank,
In single opposition hand to hand,
He did confound the best part of an hour   100
In changing hardiment with great Glendower.
Three times they breath'd, and three times did they drink,
Upon agreement, of swift Severn's flood;
Who then, affrighted with their bloody looks,
Ran fearfully among the trembling reeds   105
And hid his crisp head in the hollow bank
Bloodstained with these valiant combatants.
Never did base and rotten policy
Colour her working with such deadly wounds;
Nor never could the noble Mortimer   110
Receive so many, and all willingly.
Then let him not be slandered with revolt.
KING. Thou dost belie him, Percy, thou dost belie him;
He never did encounter with Glendower.
I tell thee   115
He durst as well have met the devil alone
As Owen Glendower for an enemy.
Art thou not asham'd? But, sirrah, henceforth
Let me not hear you speak of Mortimer;
Send me your prisoners with the speediest means,   120
Or you shall hear in such a kind from me
As will displease you. My Lord Northumberland,
We license your departure with your son.
Send us your prisoners, or you will hear of it.
            [*Exeunt* KING HENRY, BLUNT, *and* Train.   125
HOT. An if the devil come and roar for them,
I will not send them. I will after straight
And tell him so; for I will ease my heart,
Albeit I make a hazard of my head.
NORTH. What, drunk with choler? Stay and pause awhile.
Here comes your uncle.

Re-enter WORCESTER.

HOT.   Speak of Mortimer!   130
Zounds, I will speak of him; and let my soul
Want mercy if I do not join with him.
Yea, on his part I'll empty all these veins
And shed my dear blood drop by drop in the dust,
But I will lift the down-trod Mortimer   135
As high in the air as this unthankful king,
As this ingrate and cank'red Bolingbroke.
NORTH. Brother, the King hath made your nephew mad.
WOR. Who struck this heat up after I was gone?
HOT. He will, forsooth, have all my prisoners;   140

And when I urg'd the ransom once again
Of my wife's brother, then his cheek look'd pale,
And on my face he turn'd an eye of death,
Trembling even at the name of Mortimer.
WOR. I cannot blame him : was not he proclaim'd   145
  By Richard that dead is the next of blood ?
NORTH. He was : I heard the proclamation ;
  And then it was when the unhappy King—   Lines 147–187
  Whose wrongs in us God pardon !—did set forth   omitted.
  Upon his Irish expedition ;   150
  From whence he intercepted did return
  To be depos'd, and shortly murdered.
WOR. And for whose death we in the world's wide mouth
  Live scandaliz'd and foully spoken of.
HOT. But soft, I pray you : did King Richard then   155
  Proclaim my brother, Edmund Mortimer,
  Heir to the crown ?
NORTH.   He did : myself did hear it.
HOT. Nay, then I cannot blame his cousin king,
  That wish'd him on the barren mountains starve.
  But shall it be that you that set the crown   160
  Upon the head of this forgetful man,
  And for his sake wear the detested blot
  Of murderous subornation—shall it be
  That you a world of curses undergo,
  Being the agents or base second means,   165
  The cords, the ladder, or the hangman rather ?
  O, pardon me that I descend so low
  To show the line and the predicament
  Wherein you range under this subtle king !
  Shall it, for shame, be spoken in these days   170
  Or fill up chronicles in time to come,
  That men of your nobility and power
  Did gage them both in an unjust behalf—
  As both of you, God pardon it ! have done—
  To put down Richard, that sweet lovely rose,   175
  And plant this thorn, this canker, Bolingbroke ?
  And shall it, in more shame, be further spoken
  That you are fool'd, discarded, and shook off,
  By him for whom these shames ye underwent ?
  No ; yet time serves wherein you may redeem   180
  Your banish'd honours, and restore yourselves
  Into the good thoughts of the world again ;
  Revenge the jeering and disdain'd contempt
  Of this proud king, who studies day and night
  To answer all the debt he owes to you   185
  Even with the bloody payment of your deaths.
  Therefore I say—
WOR.   Peace, cousin, say no more.
  And now I will unclasp a secret book,
  And to your quick-conceiving discontents
  I'll read you matter deep and dangerous,   190
  As full of peril and adventurous spirit
  As to o'er-walk a current roaring loud

On the unsteadfast footing of a spear.
HOT. If he fall in, good night, or sink or swim.
  Send danger from the east unto the west,   195
  So honour cross it from the north to south,
  And let them grapple.   O, the blood more stirs
  To rouse a lion than to start a hare !
NORTH. Imagination of some great exploit
  Drives him beyond the bounds of patience.   200
HOT. By heaven, methinks it were an easy leap
  To pluck bright honour from the pale-fac'd moon ;
  Or dive into the bottom of the deep,
  Where fathom-line could never touch the ground,
  And pluck up drowned honour by the locks ;   205
  So he that doth redeem her thence might wear
  Without corrival all her dignities.
  But out upon this half-fac'd fellowship !
WOR. He apprehends a world of figures here,
  But not the form of what he should attend.   210
  Good cousin, give me audience for a while.
HOT. I cry you mercy.
WOR.   Those same noble Scots
  That are your prisoners—
HOT.   I'll keep them all ;
  By God, he shall not have a Scot of them ;
  No, if a Scot would save his soul, he shall not.   215
  I'll keep them, by this hand.
WOR.   You start away,
  And lend no ear unto my purposes.
  Those prisoners you shall keep.
HOT.   Nay, I will ; that's flat.
  He said he would not ransom Mortimer ;
  Forbad my tongue to speak of Mortimer ;   220
  But I will find him when he lies asleep,
  And in his ear I'll holla ' Mortimer ! '
  Nay,
  I'll have a starling shall be taught to speak
  Nothing but ' Mortimer ', and give it him   225
  To keep his anger still in motion.
WOR. Hear you, cousin ; a word.
HOT. All studies here I solemnly defy,
  Save how to gall and pinch this Bolingbroke.
  And that same sword-and-buckler Prince of Wales—   230
  But that I think his father loves him not
  And would be glad he met with some mischance—
  I would have him poison'd with a pot of ale.
WOR. Farewell, kinsman : I'll talk to you
  When you are better temper'd to attend.   235
NORTH. Why, what a wasp-stung and impatient fool
  Art thou to break into this woman's mood,
  Tying thine ear to no tongue but thine own !
HOT. Why, look you, I am whipt and scourg'd with rods,
  Nettled, and stung with pismires, when I hear   240
  Of this vile politician, Bolingbroke.
  In Richard's time—what do you call the place ?—

A plague upon it, it is in Gloucestershire—
'Twas where the madcap duke his uncle kept—
His uncle York—where I first bow'd my knee   245
Unto this king of smiles, this Bolingbroke—
'Sblood !
When you and he came back from Ravenspurgh—
NORTH. At Berkeley Castle.
HOT. You say true.   250
Why, what a candy deal of courtesy
This fawning greyhound then did proffer me !
' Look when his infant fortune came to age '
And ' gentle Harry Percy ' and ' kind cousin '—
O, the devil take such cozeners !   God forgive me   255
Good uncle, tell your tale—I have done.
WOR. Nay, if you have not, to it again ;
We will stay your leisure.
HOT.   I have done, i' faith.
WOR. Then once more to your Scottish prisoners :
Deliver them up without their ransom straight,   260
And make the Douglas' son your only mean
For powers in Scotland ; which, for divers reasons
Which I shall send you written, be assur'd
Will easily be granted. [To NORTH.]   You, my lord,
Your son in Scotland being thus employ'd,   265
Shall secretly into the bosom creep
Of that same noble prelate, well belov'd,
The Archbishop.
HOT. Of York, is it not ?
WOR. True ; who bears hard   270
His brother's death at Bristow, the Lord Scroop.
I speak not this in estimation,
As what I think might be, but what I know
Is ruminated, plotted, and set down,
And only stays but to behold the face   275
Of that occasion that shall bring it on.
HOT. I smell it.   Upon my life, it will do well.
NORTH. Before the game is afoot thou still let'st slip.
HOT. Why, it cannot choose but be a noble plot.
And then the power of Scotland and of York   280
To join with Mortimer, ha ?
WOR.   And so they shall.
HOT. In faith, it is exceedingly well aim'd.
WOR. And 'tis no little reason bids us speed,
To save our heads by raising of a head ;
For, bear ourselves as even as we can,   285
The King will always think him in our debt,
And think we think ourselves unsatisfied,
Till he hath found a time to pay us home.
And see already how he doth begin
To make us strangers to his looks of love.   290
HOT. He does, he does.   We'll be reveng'd on him.
WOR. Cousin, farewell.   No further go in this
Than I by letters shall direct your course.
When time is ripe, which will be suddenly,

I'll steal to Glendower and Lord Mortimer ;   295
Where you and Douglas and our pow'rs at once,
As I will fashion it, shall happily meet,
To bear our fortunes in our own strong arms,
Which now we hold at much uncertainty.
NORTH. Farewell, good brother. We shall thrive, I trust.   300
HOT. Uncle, adieu. O, let the hours be short
Till fields and blows and groans applaud our sport !   [*Exeunt.*

ACT TWO

SCENE I. *Rochester. An inn yard.*

Enter a Carrier *with a lantern in his hand.*

FIRST CARRIER. Heigh-ho ! an it be not four by the day, I'll be hang'd ;
Charles' wain is over the new chimney, and yet our horse not
pack'd. What, ostler !
OST. [*Within.*] Anon, anon.   4
FIRST CAR. I prithee, Tom, beat Cut's saddle ; put a few flocks in
the point ; poor jade is wrung in the withers out of all cess.

Enter another Carrier.

SEC. CAR. Peas and beans are as dank here as a dog, and that is the
next way to give poor jades the bots ; this house is turned upside
down since Robin Ostler died.   10
FIRST CAR. Poor fellow never joyed since the price of oats rose ; it
was the death of him.
SEC. CAR. I think this be the most villainous house in all London
road for fleas ; I am stung like a tench.   14
FIRST CAR. Like a tench ! By the mass, there is ne'er a king christen
could be better bit than I have been since the first cock.
SEC. CAR. Why, they will allow us ne'er a jordan ; and then we leak
in your chimney ; and your chamber-lye breeds fleas like a loach.
FIRST CAR. What, ostler ! come away, and be hang'd ; come away.
SEC. CAR. I have a gammon of bacon and two razes of ginger, to be
delivered as far as Charing Cross.   24
FIRST CAR. God's body ! the turkeys in my pannier are quite starved.
What, ostler ! A plague on thee ! hast thou never an eye in thy
head ? Canst not hear ? An 'twere not as good deed as drink
to break the pate on thee, I am a very villain. Come, and be
hang'd ! Hast no faith in thee ?   30

Enter GADSHILL.

GADS. Good morrow, carriers. What's o'clock ?
FIRST CAR. I think it be two o'clock.
GADS. I prithee lend me thy lantern to see my gelding in the stable.
FIRST CAR. Nay, by God ! Soft ! I know a trick worth two of that,
i' faith.   36
GADS. I pray thee lend me thine.
SEC. CAR. Ay, when, canst tell ? Lend me thy lantern, quoth 'a ?
Marry, I'll see thee hang'd first.
GADS. Sirrah carrier, what time do you mean to come to London ?
SEC. CAR. Time enough to go to bed with a candle, I warrant thee.

SCENE 5
Interior. Rochester.
The Stable of an Inn.
Night.
Two Carriers are
preparing for a
journey.

Line 4 omitted.

Omitted.

'Like a tench . . . like
a loach' omitted. (noted
superstition (noted
by Pliny in Natural
History, IX. 47) that
fishes are infested
with fleas

'What, ostler . . . I
warrant thee'
omitted.

Come, neighbour Mugs, we'll call up the gentlemen ; they will
along with company, for they have great charge.   45
                                                    [*Exeunt* Carriers.

GADS. What, ho ! chamberlain !

CHAM. [*Within.*] At hand, quoth pick-purse.

GADS. That's even as fair as—at hand, quoth the chamberlain ; for
thou variest no more from picking of purses than giving direction
doth from labouring ; thou layest the plot how.   51

Enter Chamberlain.

CHAM. Good morrow, Master Gadshill. It holds current that I told
you yesternight : there's a franklin in the Wild of Kent hath
brought three hundred marks with him in gold ; I heard him
tell it to one of his company last night at supper, a kind of auditor ;
one that hath abundance of charge too—God knows what. They
are up already and call for eggs and butter ; they will away
presently.

GADS. Sirrah, if they meet not with Saint Nicholas' clerks, I'll give
thee this neck.   60

CHAM. No, I'll none of it ; I pray thee keep that for the hangman ;
for I know thou worshippest Saint Nicholas as truly as a man of
falsehood may.

GADS. What talkest thou to me of the hangman ? If I hang, I'll
make a fat pair of gallows ; for if I hang, old Sir John hangs
with me ; and thou knowest he is no starveling. Tut ! there are
other Troyans that thou dream'st not of, the which for sport sake
are content to do the profession some grace ; that would, if
matters should be look'd into, for their own credit sake, make all
whole. I am joined with no foot landrakers, no long-staff sixpenny strikers, none of these mad mustachio purple-hu'd malt-
worms ; but with nobility and tranquillity, burgomasters and
great oneyers, such as can hold in, such as will strike sooner than
speak, and speak sooner than drink, and drink sooner than pray.
And yet, zounds, I lie ; for they pray continually to their saint,
the commonwealth ; or, rather, not pray to her, but prey on her ;
for they ride up and down on her, and make her their boots. 79

CHAM. What, the commonwealth their boots ? Will she hold out
water in foul way ?

GADS. She will, she will ; justice hath liquor'd her. We steal as in
a castle, cocksure ; we have the receipt of fern-seed, we walk
invisible.

CHAM. Nay, by my faith, I think you are more beholding to the night
than to fern-seed for your walking invisible.   84

GADS. Give me thy hand : thou shalt have a share in our purchase,
as I am a true man.

CHAM. Nay, rather let me have it, as you are a false thief.   95

GADS. Go to ; ' homo ' is a common name to all men. Bid the ostler
bring my gelding out of the stable. Farewell, you muddy knave.
                                                           [*Exeunt.*

PETO appears and
calls the Chamberlain
to him.
[*Within*] omitted.
'That's even . . . plot
how' omitted.

For 'Gadshill' read
'Peto'.

PETO for GADSHILL.

PETO for GADSHILL.

'such as can hold
in . . . walking
invisible' omitted.

PETO for GADSHILL.

Lines 96–97 omitted.

Yale edition reads: Trojans: a cant name for rioters

SCENE II. *The highway, near Gadshill.*

Enter the PRINCE OF WALES *and* POINS.

POINS. Come, shelter, shelter ; I have remov'd Falstaff's horse, and he frets like a gumm'd velvet.

PRINCE. Stand close.

Enter FALSTAFF.

FAL. Poins ! Poins ! And be hang'd ! Poins !

PRINCE. Peace, ye fat-kidney'd rascal ; what a brawling dost thou keep ! 6

FAL. Where's Poins, Hal ?

PRINCE. He is walk'd up to the top of the hill ; I'll go seek him.

FAL. I am accurs'd to rob in that thief's company ; the rascal hath removed my horse, and tied him I know not where. If I travel but four foot by the squier further afoot, I shall break my wind. Well, I doubt not but to die a fair death for all this, if I scape hanging for killing that rogue. I have forsworn his company hourly any time this two and twenty years, and yet I am bewitch'd with the rogue's company. If the rascal have not given me medicines to make me love him, I'll be hang'd. It could not be else : I have drunk medicines. Poins ! Hal ! A plague upon you both ! Bardolph ! Peto ! I'll starve ere I'll rob a foot further. An 'twere not as good a deed as drink to turn true man, and to leave these rogues, I am the veriest varlet that ever chewed with a tooth. Eight yards of uneven ground is three-score and ten miles afoot with me ; and the stony-hearted villains know it well enough. A plague upon it, when thieves cannot be true one to another ! [*They whistle.*] Whew ! A plague upon you all ! Give me my horse, you rogues ; give me my horse, and be hang'd. 29

PRINCE. Peace, ye fat-guts ! lie down ; lay thine ear close to the ground, and list if thou canst hear the tread of travellers.

FAL. Have you any levers to lift me up again, being down ? 'Sblood, I'll not bear mine own flesh so far afoot again for all the coin in thy father's exchequer. What a plague mean ye to colt me thus ?

PRINCE. Thou liest : thou art not colted, thou art uncolted.

FAL. I prithee, good Prince Hal, help me to my horse, good king's son.

PRINCE. Out, ye rogue ! shall I be your ostler ?

FAL. Hang thyself in thine own heir-apparent garters. If I be ta'en, I'll peach for this. An I have not ballads made on you all, and sung to filthy tunes, let a cup of sack be my poison. When a jest is so forward, and afoot too !—I hate it. 46

Enter GADSHILL, BARDOLPH *and* PETO *with him.*

GADS. Stand !

FAL. So I do, against my will.

POINS. O, 'tis our setter : I know his voice. Bardolph, what news ?

BARD. Case ye, case ye ; on with your vizards : there's money of the King's coming down the hill ; 'tis going to the King's exchequer.

FAL. You lie, ye rogue ; 'tis going to the King's tavern.

GADS. There's enough to make us all. 55

FAL. To be hang'd.

SCENE 6
Exterior. A Country Road near Gadshill. Almost Dawn.

'Well, I doubt not . . . drunk medicines' omitted.

'And 'twere not . . . with a tooth' omitted.

'When a jest . . . I hate it' omitted.
Omit Gadshill.
PETO for GADSHILL.

'Bardolph, what news?' omitted.

PETO for GADSHILL.

PRINCE. Sirs, you four shall front them in the narrow lane; Ned
   Poins and I will walk lower; if they scape from your encounter,
   then they light on us.
PETO. How many be there of them?   60
GADS. Some eight or ten.
FAL. Zounds, will they not rob us?
PRINCE. What, a coward, Sir John Paunch?
FAL. Indeed, I am not John of Gaunt, your grandfather; but yet
   no coward, Hal.   65
PRINCE. Well, we leave that to the proof.
POINS. Sirrah Jack, thy horse stands behind the hedge: when thou
   need'st him, there thou shalt find him. Farewell, and stand fast.
FAL. Now cannot I strike him, if I should be hang'd.   70
PRINCE. [*Aside to* POINS.] Ned, where are our disguises?
POINS. [*Aside.*] Here, hard by; stand close.
                [*Exeunt the* PRINCE *and* POINS.
FAL. Now, my masters, happy man be his dole, say I; every man
   to his business.

            Enter the Travellers.

FIRST TRAV. Come, neighbour; the boy shall lead our horses down
   the hill; we'll walk afoot awhile, and ease our legs.
THIEVES. Stand!
TRAVELLERS. Jesus bless us!   79
FAL. Strike; down with them; cut the villains' throats. Ah,
   whoreson caterpillars! bacon-fed knaves! They hate us youth.
   Down with them; fleece them.
TRAV. O, we are undone, both we and ours for ever!
FAL. Hang ye, gorbellied knaves, are ye undone? No, ye fat chuffs;
   I would your store were here. On, bacons, on! What, ye
   knaves! young men must live. You are grand-jurors, are ye?
   we'll jure ye, faith. [*Here they rob them and bind them. Exeunt.*

    Re-enter the PRINCE *and* POINS *in buckram.*

PRINCE. The thieves have bound the true men. Now, could thou
   and I rob the thieves and go merrily to London, it would be
   argument for a week, laughter for a month, and a good jest for
   ever.   92
POINS. Stand close; I hear them coming.

      Enter the Thieves *again.*

FAL. Come, my masters, let us share, and then to horse before day.
   An the Prince and Poins be not two arrant cowards, there's no
   equity stirring. There's no more valour in that Poins than in
   a wild duck.   97
      [*As they are sharing, the* PRINCE *and* POINS *set upon them.*
PRINCE. Your money!
POINS. Villains!
[*They all run away, and* FALSTAFF, *after a blow or two, runs away too,*
              leaving the booty behind them.
PRINCE. Got with much ease. Now merrily to horse.   100
   The thieves are all scattered, and possess'd with fear
   So strongly that they dare not meet each other;

Marginal notes (right column):

For 'four' read 'three'.

BARDOLPH for PETO.
PETO for GADSHILL.

Lines 75–79 omitted.

'fleece them . . . we'll
jure ye, faith'
omitted.

Lines 88–93 omitted.

Omitted.

'share, and then'
omitted.

Lines 100–104,
'Away, good Ned,'
omitted.

Jon Finch as Henry IV with (from left) Prince John of Lancaster (Rob Edwards), Prince Hal (David Gwillim) and the Earl of Westmoreland (David Buck)

Anthony Quayle as Sir John Falstaff with Poins (Jack Galloway) and Prince Hal

*Michele Dotrice as Lady Percy and Tim
Pigott-Smith as Hotspur*

David Neal as Scroop, Archbishop of York

Jon Finch as King Henry IV

Glendower (Richard Owens) with Lady Mortimer (Sharon Morgan) and Mortimer (Robert Morris)

Anthony Quayle as Falstaff with Bardolph (Gordon Gostelow) and the boy (John Fowler)

Hotspur (Tim Pigott-Smith) is killed by Prince Hal (David Gwillim)

Each takes his fellow for an officer.
Away, good Ned. Falstaff sweats to death
And lards the lean earth as he walks along.   105
Were't not for laughing, I should pity him.
POINS. How the fat rogue roar'd !   [*Exeunt.*

SCENE III. *Warkworth Castle.*

Enter HOTSPUR *solus, reading a letter.*

HOT. ' But, for mine own part, my lord, I could be well contented
to be there, in respect of the love I bear your house.' He could
be contented—why is he not, then ? In respect of the love he
bears our house—he shows in this he loves his own barn better
than he loves our house. Let me see some more. ' The purpose
you undertake is dangerous '—why, that's certain : 'tis dangerous
to take a cold, to sleep, to drink ; but I tell you, my lord fool, out
of this nettle, danger, we pluck this flower, safety. ' The purpose
you undertake is dangerous ; the friends you have named uncertain ; the time itself unsorted ; and your whole plot too light
for the counterpoise of so great an opposition.' Say you so, say
you so ? I say unto you again, you are a shallow, cowardly hind,
and you lie. What a lack-brain is this ! By the Lord, our plot
is a good plot as ever was laid ; our friends true and constant—a
good plot, good friends, and full of expectation ; an excellent
plot, very good friends. What a frosty-spirited rogue is this !
Why, my Lord of York commends the plot and the general course
of the action. Zounds, an I were now by this rascal, I could
brain him with his lady's fan. Is there not my father, my uncle,
and myself ; Lord Edmund Mortimer, my Lord of York, and
Owen Glendower ? Is there not, besides, the Douglas ? Have
I not all their letters to meet me in arms by the ninth of the
next month, and are they not some of them set forward already ?
What a pagan rascal is this ! an infidel ! Ha ! you shall see now,
in very sincerity of fear and cold heart, will he to the King and
lay open all our proceedings. O, I could divide myself and go
to buffets for moving such a dish of skim milk with so honourable
an action ! Hang him ; let him tell the King : we are prepared.
I will set forward to-night.   32

Enter LADY PERCY.

How now, Kate ! I must leave you within these two hours.
LADY. O my good lord, why are you thus alone ?
For what offence have I this fortnight been   35
A banish'd woman from my Harry's bed ?
Tell me, sweet lord, what is't that takes from thee
Thy stomach, pleasure, and thy golden sleep ?
Why dost thou bend thine eyes upon the earth,
And start so often when thou sit'st alone ?   40
Why hast thou lost the fresh blood in thy cheeks,
And given my treasures and my rights of thee
To thick-ey'd musing and curs'd melancholy ?
In thy faint slumbers I by thee have watch'd,
And heard thee murmur tales of iron wars ;   45

*The historical Lady
Percy was named
Elizabeth*

49

Speak terms of manage to thy bounding steed ;
Cry ' Courage !   To the field ! '   And thou hast talk'd
Of sallies and retires, of trenches, tents,
Of palisadoes, frontiers, parapets,
Of basilisks, of cannon, culverin,   50
Of prisoners' ransom, and of soldiers slain,
And all the currents of a heady fight.
Thy spirit within thee hath been so at war,
And thus hath so bestirr'd thee in thy sleep,
That beads of sweat have stood upon thy brow   55
Like bubbles in a late disturbed stream ;
And in thy face strange motions have appear'd,
Such as we see when men restrain their breath
On some great sudden hest.   O, what portents are these ?
Some heavy business hath my lord in hand,   60
And I must know it, else he loves me not.
HOT. What, ho !

Enter a Servant.

                  Is Gilliams with the packet gone ?
SERV. He is, my lord, an hour ago.
HOT. Hath Butler brought those horses from the sheriff ?
SERV. One horse, my lord, he brought even now.   65
HOT. What horse ?   A roan, a crop-ear, is it not ?
SERV. It is, my lord.
HOT.   That roan shall be my throne.
Well, I will back him straight.   O esperance !
Bid Butler lead him forth into the park.   [*Exit* Servant. | Line 69 omitted.
LADY. But hear you, my lord.   70
HOT. What say'st thou, my lady ?
LADY. What is it carries you away ?
HOT. Why, my horse, my love, my horse.
LADY. Out, you mad-headed ape !
A weasel hath not such a deal of spleen   75
As you are toss'd with.   In faith,
I'll know your business, Harry, that I will.
I fear my brother Mortimer doth stir
About his title and hath sent for you
To line his enterprise ; but if you go—   80
HOT. So far afoot, I shall be weary, love.
LADY. Come, come, you paraquito, answer me
Directly unto this question that I ask.
In faith, I'll break thy little finger, Harry,
An if thou wilt not tell me all things true.   85
HOT. Away.
Away, you trifler !   Love, I love thee not,
I care not for thee, Kate ; this is no world
To play with mammets and to tilt with lips :
We must have bloody noses and crack'd crowns,   90
And pass them current too.   God's me, my horse !
What say'st thou, Kate ? what wouldst thou have with me ?
LADY. Do you not love me ?   Do you not, indeed ?
Well, do not, then ; for since you love me not,
I will not love myself.   Do you not love me ?   95

Nay, tell me if you speak in jest or no.
HOT. Come, wilt thou see me ride?
And when I am o' horseback, I will swear
I love thee infinitely. But hark you, Kate:
I must not have you henceforth question me   100
Whither I go, nor reason whereabout.
Whither I must, I must; and, to conclude,
This evening must I leave you, gentle Kate.
I know you wise, but yet no farther wise
Than Harry Percy's wife; constant you are,   105
But yet a woman; and for secrecy,
No lady closer; for I well believe
Thou wilt not utter what thou dost not know,
And so far will I trust thee, gentle Kate.
LADY. How, so far?   110
HOT. Not an inch further. But hark you, Kate:
Whither I go, thither shall you go too;
To-day will I set forth, to-morrow you.
Will this content you, Kate?
LADY.   It must, of force.   [*Exeunt.*

SCENE IV. *Eastcheap. The Boar's Head Tavern.*

Enter the PRINCE, *and* POINS.

PRINCE. Ned, prithee, come out of that fat room and lend me thy
hand to laugh a little.
POINS. Where hast been, Hal?
PRINCE. With three or four loggerheads amongst three or fourscore
hogsheads. I have sounded the very base-string of humility.
Sirrah, I am sworn brother to a leash of drawers and can call
them all by their christen names, as Tom, Dick, and Francis.
They take it already upon their salvation that though I be but
Prince of Wales yet I am the king of courtesy; and tell me flatly
I am no proud Jack, like Falstaff, but a Corinthian, a lad of
mettle, a good boy—by the Lord, so they call me—and when
I am King of England I shall command all the good lads in
Eastcheap. They call drinking deep, dyeing scarlet; and when
you breathe in your watering, they cry 'hem!' and bid you play
it off.   To conclude, I am so good a proficient in one quarter of
an hour that I can drink with any tinker in his own language
during my life. I tell thee, Ned, thou hast lost much honour
that thou wert not with me in this action. But, sweet Ned—to
sweeten which name of Ned, I give thee this pennyworth of
sugar, clapp'd even now into my hand by an under-skinker, one
that never spake other English in his life than ' Eight shillings
and sixpence' and 'You are welcome' with this shrill addition,
'Anon, anon, sir! Score a pint of bastard in the Half-moon'
or so. But, Ned, to drive away the time till Falstaff come, I
prithee, do thou stand in some by-room, while I question my
puny drawer to what end he gave me the sugar; and do thou
never leave calling ' Francis!' that his tale to me may be nothing
but 'Anon'. Step aside, and I'll show thee a precedent.   31
                                                      [*Exit* POINS.
POINS. [*Within.*] Francis!

SCENE 8
*Interior. Eastcheap.
The Boar's Head
Tavern. Night.*

Lines 13–77, 'They
call drinking deep
. . . My Lord, old',
omitted.

PRINCE. Thou are perfect.
POINS. [*Within.*]   Francis!

Lines 13–77, 'They call drinking deep . . . My lord, old', omitted.

Enter FRANCIS.

FRAN. Anon, anon, sir.   Look down into the Pomgarnet, Ralph.
PRINCE. Come thither, Francis.
FRAN. My lord?
PRINCE. How long hast thou to serve, Francis?
FRAN. Forsooth, five years, and as much as to—   40
POINS. [*Within.*]   Francis!
FRAN. Anon, anon, sir.
PRINCE. Five year! by'r lady, a long lease for the clinking of pewter.
   But, Francis, darest thou be so valiant as to play the coward with
   thy indenture and show it a fair pair of heels and run from it?
FRAN. O Lord, sir, I'll be sworn upon all the books in England, I
   could find in my heart—
POINS. [*Within.*]   Francis!
FRAN. Anon, sir.   50
PRINCE. How old art thou, Francis?
FRAN. Let me see, about Michaelmas next I shall be—
POINS. [*Within.*]   Francis!
FRAN. Anon, sir.   Pray stay a little, my lord.
PRINCE. Nay, but hark you, Francis: for the sugar thou gavest me—
   'twas a pennyworth, was't not?   56
FRAN. O Lord, I would it had been two!
PRINCE. I will give thee for it a thousand pound; ask me when thou
   wilt, and thou shalt have it.
POINS. [*Within.*]   Francis!   60
FRAN. Anon, anon.
PRINCE. Anon, Francis? No, Francis; but to-morrow, Francis;
   or, Francis, o' Thursday; or indeed, Francis, when thou wilt.
   But, Francis—
FRAN. My lord?   65
PRINCE. Wilt thou rob this leathern jerkin, crystal-button, knot-pated,
   agate-ring, puke-stocking, caddis-garter, smooth-tongue, Spanish-
   pouch—
FRAN. O Lord, sir, who do you mean?   69
PRINCE. Why, then, your brown bastard is your only drink; for,
   look you, Francis, your white canvas doublet will sully. In
   Barbary, sir, it cannot come to so much.
FRAN. What, sir?
POINS. [*Within.*]   Francis!   74
PRINCE. Away, you rogue!   Dost thou not hear them call?
[*Here they both call him;* FRANCIS *stands amazed, not knowing which
                                                      way to go.*

Enter Vintner.

A drawer enters.

VINT. What, stand'st thou still, and hear'st such a calling? Look
   to the guests within. [*Exit* FRANCIS.] My lord, old Sir John,
   with half-a-dozen more, are at the door. Shall I let them in?

DRAWER for VINTNER.

PRINCE. Let them alone awhile, and then open the door. [*Exit*
   Vintner.]   Poins!   82

'and then open the door . . . what's the issue?' omitted.

Re-enter POINS.

POINS. Anon, anon, sir.
PRINCE. Sirrah, Falstaff and the rest of the thieves are at the door.
　　Shall we be merry ?   85
POINS. As merry as crickets, my lad. But hark ye : what cunning
　　match have you made with this jest of the drawer ? Come,
　　what's the issue ?
PRINCE. I am now of all humours that have showed themselves
　　humours since the old days of goodman Adam to the pupil-age
　　of this present twelve o'clock at midnight.   92

'and then open the
door . . . what's the
issue?' omitted.

Re-enter FRANCIS.

Omitted.

　　What's o'clock, Francis ?
FRAN. Anon, anon, sir.   [*Exit.*
PRINCE. That ever this fellow should have fewer words than a parrot,
　　and yet the son of a woman ! His industry is upstairs and down-
　　stairs ; his eloquence the parcel of a reckoning. I am not yet
　　of Percy's mind, the Hotspur of the north ; he that kills me
　　some six or seven dozen of Scots at a breakfast, washes his hands,
　　and says to his wife ' Fie upon this quiet life ! I want work'.
　　' O my sweet Harry,' says she ' how many hast thou kill'd to-day ? '
　　' Give my roan horse a drench ' says he ; and answers ' Some
　　fourteen,' an hour after, ' a trifle, a trifle'. I prithee call in
　　Falstaff ; I'll play Percy, and that damn'd brawn shall play
　　Dame Mortimer his wife. ' Rivo ! ' says the drunkard. Call in
　　ribs, call in tallow.

'What's o'clock . . .
parcel of a reckoning'
omitted.

Enter FALSTAFF, GADSHILL, BARDOLPH, *and* PETO ; *followed by* FRANCIS
with wine.

Omit Gadshill and
Francis.

POINS. Welcome, Jack. Where hast thou been ?   108
FAL. A plague of all cowards, I say, and a vengeance too ! Marry
　　and amen ! Give me a cup of sack, boy. Ere I lead this life
　　long, I'll sew nether-stocks, and mend them and foot them too.
　　A plague of all cowards ! Give me a cup of sack, rogue. Is
　　there no virtue extant ?   [*He drinks.*
PRINCE. Didst thou never see Titan kiss a dish of butter, pitiful-
　　hearted Titan, that melted at the sweet tale of the sun's ? If
　　thou didst, then behold that compound.   116
FAL. You rogue, here's lime in this sack too ! There is nothing but
　　roguery to be found in villainous man ; yet a coward is worse
　　than a cup of sack with lime in it. A villainous coward ! Go
　　thy ways, old Jack ; die when thou wilt ; if manhood, good
　　manhood, be not forgot upon the face of the earth, then am I
　　a shotten herring. There lives not three good men unhang'd in
　　England, and one of them is fat and grows old. God help the
　　while ! A bad world, I say. I would I were a weaver ; I could
　　sing psalms or anything. A plague of all cowards, I say still.
PRINCE. How now, woolsack ! What mutter you ?   128
FAL. A king's son ! If I do not beat thee out of thy kingdom with
　　a dagger of lath, and drive all thy subjects afore thee like a flock
　　of wild geese, I'll never wear hair on my face more. You Prince
　　of Wales !   132
PRINCE. Why, you whoreson round man, what's the matter ?
FAL. Are not you a coward ? Answer me to that—and Poins there ?

POINS. Zounds, ye fat paunch, an ye call me coward, by the Lord,
I'll stab thee.   138
FAL. I call thee coward! I'll see thee damn'd ere I call thee coward;
but I would give a thousand pound I could run as fast as thou
canst. You are straight enough in the shoulders—you care not
who sees your back. Call you that backing of your friends?
A plague upon such backing! Give me them that will face me.
Give me a cup of sack; I am a rogue if I drunk to-day.   145
PRINCE. O villain! thy lips are scarce wip'd since thou drunk'st last.
FAL. All is one for that. [*He drinks.*] A plague of all cowards, still
say I.
PRINCE. What's the matter?
FAL. What's the matter! There be four of us here have ta'en a   For 'four' read
thousand pound this day morning.   'three'.
PRINCE. Where is it, Jack? Where is it?
FAL. Where is it! taken from us it is: a hundred upon poor four   For 'four' read
of us.   155   'three'.
PRINCE. What, a hundred, man?
FAL. I am a rogue if I were not at half-sword with a dozen of them
two hours together. I have scap'd by miracle. I am eight
times thrust through the doublet, four through the hose; my
buckler cut through and through; my sword hack'd like a
hand-saw—ecce signum! I never dealt better since I was a
man—all would not do. A plague of all cowards! Let them
speak; if they speak more or less than truth, they are villains
and the sons of darkness.   165
PRINCE. Speak, sirs; how was it?
GADS. We four set upon some dozen—   PETO. For 'four'
FAL. Sixteen at least, my lord.   read 'three'.
GADS. And bound them.   FALSTAFF for GADSHILL.
PETO. No, no, they were not bound.   170
FAL. You rogue, they were bound, every man of them; or I am a
Jew else, an Ebrew Jew.
GADS. As we were sharing, some six or seven fresh men set upon us—   PETO for GADSHILL.
FAL. And unbound the rest, and then come in the other.
PRINCE. What, fought you with them all?
FAL. All! I know not what you call all, but if I fought not with
fifty of them, I am a bunch of radish. If there were not two or
three and fifty upon poor old Jack, then am I no two-legg'd
creature.   181
PRINCE. Pray God you have not murd'red some of them.
FAL. Nay, that's past praying for: I have pepper'd two of them;
two I am sure I have paid—two rogues in buckram suits. I tell
thee what, Hal, if I tell thee a lie, spit in my face, call me horse.
Thou knowest my old ward: here I lay, and thus I bore my
point. Four rogues in buckram let drive at me—   189
PRINCE. What, four? Thou saidst but two even now.
FAL. Four, Hal; I told thee four.
POINS. Ay, ay, he said four.
FAL. These four came all afront, and mainly thrust at me. I made
me no more ado but took all their seven points in my target, thus.
PRINCE. Seven? Why, there were but four even now.   196
FAL. In buckram.
POINS. Ay, four, in buckram suits.

FAL. Seven, by these hilts, or I am a villain else.
PRINCE. [*Aside to* POINS.] Prithee, let him alone; we shall have
  more anon.   201
FAL. Dost thou hear me, Hal?
PRINCE. Ay, and mark thee too, Jack.
FAL. Do so, for it is worth the list'ning to. These nine in buckram
  that I told thee of—
PRINCE. So, two more already.
FAL. Their points being broken—
POINS. Down fell their hose.   208
FAL. Began to give me ground; but I followed me close, came in
  foot and hand, and with a thought seven of the eleven I paid.
PRINCE. O monstrous! eleven buckram men grown out of two!
FAL. But, as the devil would have it, three misbegotten knaves in
  Kendal green came at my back and let drive at me—for it was
  so dark, Hal, that thou couldest not see thy hand.   217
PRINCE. These lies are like their father that begets them—gross as a
  mountain, open, palpable. Why, thou clay-brain'd guts, thou
  knotty-pated fool, thou whoreson, obscene, greasy tallow-catch—
FAL. What, art thou mad? art thou mad?
  Is not the truth the truth?
PRINCE. Why, how couldst thou know these men in Kendal green,
  when it was so dark thou couldst not see thy hand? Come,
  tell us your reason; what sayest thou to this?   227
POINS. Come, your reason, Jack, your reason.
FAL. What, upon compulsion? Zounds, an I were at the strappado,
  or all the racks in the world, I would not tell you on compulsion.
  Give you a reason on compulsion! If reasons were as plentiful
  as blackberries, I would give no man a reason upon compulsion, I.
PRINCE. I'll be no longer guilty of this sin; this sanguine coward,
  this bed-presser, this horse-back-breaker, this huge hill of flesh—
FAL. 'Sblood, you starveling, you eel-skin, you dried neat's-tongue,
  you bull's pizzle, you stock-fish—O for breath to utter what is
  like thee!—you tailor's yard, you sheath, you bow-case, you vile
  standing tuck!   240
PRINCE. Well, breathe awhile, and then to it again; and when thou
  hast tired thyself in base comparisons, hear me speak but this.
POINS. Mark, Jack.
PRINCE. We two saw you four set on four, and bound them and were
  masters of their wealth. Mark now, how a plain tale shall put
  you down. Then did we two set on you four; and, with a word,
  out-fac'd you from your prize, and have it; yea, and can show
  it you here in the house. And, Falstaff, you carried your guts
  away as nimbly, with as quick dexterity, and roar'd for mercy,
  and still run and roar'd, as ever I heard bull-calf. What a slave
  art thou to hack thy sword as thou hast done, and then say it
  was in fight! What trick, what device, what starting-hole, canst
  thou now find out to hide thee from this open and apparent
  shame?   256
POINS. Come, let's hear, Jack; what trick hast thou now?
FAL. By the Lord, I knew ye as well as he that made ye. Why,
  hear you, my masters: was it for me to kill the heir-apparent?
  Should I turn upon the true prince? Why, thou knowest I am
  as valiant as Hercules; but beware instinct—the lion will not

For 'four' read
'three'. 'and bound
them' omitted. For
'four' read 'three'.

touch the true prince. Instinct is a great matter : I was now a
coward on instinct. I shall think the better of myself and thee
during my life—I for a valiant lion, and thou for a true prince.
But, by the Lord, lads, I am glad you have the money. Hostess,
clap to the doors. Watch to-night, pray to-morrow. Gallants,
lads, boys, hearts of gold, all the titles of good fellowship come
to you ! What, shall we be merry ? Shall we have a play
extempore ?   271
PRINCE. Content—and the argument shall be thy running away.
FAL. Ah, no more of that, Hal, an thou lovest me !

Enter Hostess.

HOST. O Jesu, my lord the Prince !   275
PRINCE. How now, my lady the hostess !
What say'st thou to me ?
HOST. Marry, my lord, there is a nobleman of the court at door
would speak with you ; he says he comes from your father.
PRINCE. Give him as much as will make him a royal man, and send
him back again to my mother.
FAL. What manner of man is he ?
HOST. An old man.
FAL. What doth gravity out of his bed at midnight ? Shall I give
him his answer ?   286
PRINCE. Prithee do, Jack.
FAL. Faith, and I'll send him packing.   [*Exit.*
PRINCE. Now, sirs : by'r lady, you fought fair ; so did you, Peto ;
so did you, Bardolph. You are lions too : you ran away upon | 'so did you' omitted.
instinct ; you will not touch the true prince ; no, fie !   292
BARD. Faith, I ran when I saw others run.
PRINCE. Faith, tell me now in earnest, how came Falstaff's sword so
hack'd ?
PETO. Why, he hack'd it with his dagger, and said he would swear
truth out of England but he would make you believe it was done
in fight ; and persuaded us to do the like.   299
BARD. Yea, and to tickle our noses with spear-grass to make them
bleed, and then to beslubber our garments with it, and swear it
was the blood of true men. I did that I did not this seven year
before—I blush'd to hear his monstrous devices.   304
PRINCE. O villain ! Thou stolest a cup of sack eighteen years ago,
and wert taken with the manner, and ever since thou hast blush'd
extempore. Thou hadst fire and sword on thy side, and yet | Lines 307, 'Thou
thou ran'st away ; what instinct hadst thou for it ?   309 | hadst fire . . .', to 316
BARD. My lord, do you see these meteors ? do you behold these | omitted.
exhalations ?
PRINCE. I do.
BARD. What think you they portend ?
PRINCE. Hot livers and cold purses.
BARD. Choler, my lord, if rightly taken.   315
PRINCE. No, if rightly taken, halter.

Re-enter FALSTAFF.

Here comes lean Jack, here comes bare-bone. How now, my | FALSTAFF is
sweet creature of bombast ! How long is't ago, Jack, since thou | accompanied by the
sawest thine own knee ?   319 | HOSTESS and a crowd
                                                                 | of customers.

FAL. My own knee! When I was about thy years, Hal, I was not
an eagle's talon in the waist: I could have crept into any alder-
man's thumb-ring. A plague of sighing and grief! it blows a
man up like a bladder. There's villainous news abroad. Here
was Sir John Bracy from your father: you must to the court
in the morning. That same mad fellow of the north, Percy, and
he of Wales that gave Amaimon the bastinado, and made Lucifer
cuckold, and swore the devil his true liegeman upon the cross of
a Welsh hook—what a plague call you him?

POINS. O, Glendower.   330

FAL. Owen, Owen—the same; and his son-in-law Mortimer, and
old Northumberland, and that sprightly Scot of Scots, Douglas,
that runs o' horseback up a hill perpendicular—

PRINCE. He that rides at high speed and with his pistol kills a sparrow
flying?

FAL. You have hit it.

PRINCE. So did he never the sparrow.

FAL. Well, that rascal hath good mettle in him; he will not run.

PRINCE. Why, what a rascal art thou, then, to praise him so for
running!

FAL. O' horseback, ye cuckoo; but afoot he will not budge a foot.

PRINCE. Yes, Jack, upon instinct.   345

FAL. I grant ye, upon instinct. Well, he is there too, and one
Mordake, and a thousand blue-caps more. Worcester is stol'n
away to-night; thy father's beard is turn'd white with the news;
you may buy land now as cheap as stinking mack'rel.   350

PRINCE. Why, then, it is like, if there come a hot June, and this civil
buffeting hold, we shall buy maidenheads as they buy hob-nails,
by the hundreds.

FAL. By the mass, lad, thou sayest true: it is like we shall have good
trading that way. But tell me, Hal, art not thou horrible afeard.
Thou being heir-apparent, could the world pick thee out three
such enemies again as that fiend Douglas, that spirit Percy, and
that devil Glendower? Art thou not horribly afraid? Doth
not thy blood thrill at it?   360

PRINCE. Not a whit, i' faith; I lack some of thy instinct.

FAL. Well, thou wilt be horribly chid to-morrow when thou comest
to thy father. If thou love me, practise an answer.

PRINCE. Do thou stand for my father, and examine me upon the
particulars of my life.

FAL. Shall I? Content! This chair shall be my state, this dagger
my sceptre, and this cushion my crown.

PRINCE. Thy state is taken for a join'd-stool, thy golden sceptre for
a leaden dagger, and thy precious rich crown for a pitiful bald
crown!   371

FAL. Well, an the fire of grace be not quite out of thee, now shalt
thou be moved. Give me a cup of sack to make my eyes look
red, that it may be thought I have wept; for I must speak in
passion, and I will do it in King Cambyses' vein.   376

PRINCE. Well, here is my leg.

FAL. And here is my speech. Stand aside, nobility.

HOST. O Jesu, this is excellent sport, i' faith!

FAL. Weep not, sweet queen, for trickling tears are vain.

HOST. O, the father, how he holds his countenance!

'and this civil
buffeting hold'
omitted.

'Thy state is . . . thou
be moved' omitted.

'for I must . . . is my
speech' omitted.

FAL. For God's sake, lords, convey my tristful queen ;
For tears do stop the floodgates of her eyes.
HOST. O Jesu, he doth it as like one of these harlotry players as ever
I see !   385
FAL. Peace, good pint-pot ; peace, good tickle-brain.—Harry, I do
not only marvel where thou spendest thy time, but also how thou
art accompanied ; for though the camomile, the more it is trodden
on the faster it grows, yet youth, the more it is wasted the sooner
it wears. That thou art my son I have partly thy mother's word,
partly my own opinion, but chiefly a villainous trick of thine eye,
and a foolish hanging of thy nether lip, that doth warrant me.
If then thou be son to me, here lies the point : why, being son
to me, art thou so pointed at ? Shall the blessed sun of heaven
prove a micher and eat blackberries ? A question not to be
ask'd. Shall the son of England prove a thief and take purses ?
A question to be ask'd. There is a thing, Harry, which thou
hast often heard of, and it is known to many in our land by the
name of pitch. This pitch, as ancient writers do report, doth
defile ; so doth the company thou keepest ; for, Harry, now I
do not speak to thee in drink, but in tears ; not in pleasure, but
in passion ; not in words only, but in woes also. And yet there
is a virtuous man whom I have often noted in thy company, but
I know not his name.   406
PRINCE. What manner of man, an it like your Majesty ?
FAL. A goodly portly man, i' faith, and a corpulent ; of a cheerful
look, a pleasing eye, and a most noble carriage ; and, as I think,
his age some fifty, or, by 'r lady, inclining to three-score. And
now I remember me, his name is Falstaff. If that man should
be lewdly given, he deceiveth me ; for, Harry, I see virtue in
his looks. If then the tree may be known by the fruit, as the
fruit by the tree, then, peremptorily I speak it, there is virtue in
that Falstaff : him keep with, the rest banish. And tell me now,
thou naughty varlet, tell me, where hast thou been this month ?
PRINCE. Dost thou speak like a king ? Do thou stand for me, and
I'll play my father.   419
FAL. Depose me ? If thou dost it half so gravely, so majestically,
both in word and matter, hang me up by the heels for a rabbit-
sucker or a poulter's hare.
PRINCE. Well, here I am set.
FAL. And here I stand. Judge, my masters.
PRINCE. Now, Harry, whence come you ?   425
FAL. My noble lord, from Eastcheap.
PRINCE. The complaints I hear of thee are grievous.
FAL. 'Sblood, my lord, they are false. Nay, I'll tickle ye for a young
prince, i' faith.   429
PRINCE. Swearest thou, ungracious boy ? Henceforth ne'er look on
me. Thou art violently carried away from grace ; there is a
devil haunts thee in the likeness of an old fat man ; a tun of man
is thy companion. Why dost thou converse with that trunk of
humours, that bolting-hutch of beastliness, that swoll'n parcel of
dropsies, that huge bombard of sack, that stuff'd cloak-bag of
guts, that roasted Manningtree ox with the pudding in his belly,
that reverend vice, that grey iniquity, that father ruffian, that
vanity in years ? Wherein is he good, but to taste sack and

'for though the
camomile . . . A
question to be ask'd'
omitted.

After 'his name is
Falstaff' HOSTESS
says: 'Falstaff!'

58

drink it ? wherein neat and cleanly, but to carve a capon and eat
it ? wherein cunning, but in craft ? wherein crafty, but in villainy ?
wherein villainous, but in all things ? wherein worthy, but in
nothing ?

FAL. I would your Grace would take me with you ; whom means
your Grace ?   445

PRINCE. That villainous abominable misleader of youth, Falstaff, that
old white-bearded Satan.

FAL. My lord, the man I know.

PRINCE. I know thou dost.

FAL. But to say I know more harm in him than in myself were to
say more than I know. That he is old—the more the pity—his
white hairs do witness it ; but that he is—saving your reverence—
a whoremaster, that I utterly deny. If sack and sugar be a fault,
God help the wicked ! If to be old and merry be a sin, then
many an old host that I know is damn'd ; if to be fat be to be hated,
then Pharaoh's lean kine are to be loved. No, my good lord :
banish Peto, banish Bardolph, banish Poins ; but, for sweet
Jack Falstaff, kind Jack Falstaff, true Jack Falstaff, valiant Jack
Falstaff—and therefore more valiant, being, as he is, old Jack
Falstaff—banish not him thy Harry's company, banish not him
thy Harry's company. Banish plump Jack, and banish all the
world.   463

PRINCE. I do, I will.   [A knocking heard.

[Exeunt Hostess, FRANCIS, and BARDOLPH.

Re-enter BARDOLPH, running.

Omit Francis.
BARDOLPH runs to a
window and looks
out.

BARD. O, my lord, my lord ! the sheriff with a most monstrous watch
is at the door.   466

FAL. Out, ye rogue ! Play out the play : I have much to say in the
behalf of that Falstaff.

Re-enter the Hostess.

HOST. O Jesu, my lord, my lord !

PRINCE. Heigh, heigh ! the devil rides upon a fiddle-stick ; what's
the matter ?   471

HOST. The sheriff and all the watch are at the door ; they are come
to search the house. Shall I let them in ?

FAL. Dost thou hear, Hal ? Never call a true piece of gold a counterfeit. Thou art essentially made, without seeming so.   476

PRINCE. And thou a natural coward, without instinct.

FAL. I deny your major. If you will deny the sheriff, so ; if not,
let him enter. If I become not a cart as well as another man,
a plague on my bringing up ! I hope I shall as soon be strangled
with a halter as another.   481

PRINCE. Go, hide thee behind the arras ; the rest walk up above.
Now, my masters, for a true face and good conscience.

FAL. Both which I have had ; but their date is out, and therefore
I'll hide me.   [Exeunt all but the PRINCE and PETO.

For 'PETO' read
'POINS'.

PRINCE. Call in the sheriff.

Enter Sheriff and the Carrier.

Now, master sheriff, what is your will with me ?

SHER. First, pardon me, my lord. A hue and cry

Hath followed certain men unto this house.   490
PRINCE. What men?
SHER. One of them is well known, my gracious lord—
A gross fat man.
CAR. As fat as butter.
PRINCE. The man, I do assure you, is not here,
For I myself at this time have employ'd him.   495
And, sheriff, I will engage my word to thee
That I will, by to-morrow dinner-time,
Send him to answer thee, or any man,
For any thing he shall be charg'd withal;
And so let me entreat you leave the house.   500
SHER. I will, my lord. There are two gentlemen
Have in this robbery lost three hundred marks.
PRINCE. It may be so; if he have robb'd these men
He shall be answerable; and so, farewell.
SHER. Good night, my noble lord.   505
PRINCE. I think it is good morrow, is it not?
SHER. Indeed, my lord, I think it be two o'clock.
                    [*Exeunt* Sheriff *and* Carrier.
PRINCE. This oily rascal is known as well as Paul's. Go, call him
forth.   509
PETO. Falstaff! Fast asleep behind the arras, and snorting like a   POINS for PETO.
horse.
PRINCE. Hark how hard he fetches breath. Search his pockets.
[*He searcheth his pocket, and findeth certain papers.*] What hast
thou found?
PETO. Nothing but papers, my lord.   515   POINS for PETO.
PRINCE. Let's see what they be: read them.
PETO. [*Reads.*]   POINS for PETO.

Item, A capon	–	–	–	–	–	–	–	2s.	2d.
Item, Sauce	–	–	–	–	–		4d.
Item, Sack, two gallons	–	–	–	–	5s.	8d.
Item, Anchovies and sack after supper	–	–	–	2s.	6d.
Item, Bread	–	–	–	–	–	–		ob.

PRINCE. O monstrous! but one halfpennyworth of bread to this
intolerable deal of sack! What there is else, keep close; we'll
read it at more advantage. There let him sleep till day. I'll
to the court in the morning. We must all to the wars, and thy
place shall be honourable. I'll procure this fat rogue a charge   For 'Peto' read
of foot; and I know his death will be a march of twelve-score.   'Ned'.
The money shall be paid back again with advantage. Be with
me betimes in the morning; and so, good morrow, Peto. 530
PETO. Good morrow, good my lord.   [*Exeunt.*   POINS for PETO.

ACT THREE

SCENE I. *Wales. Glendower's castle.*

Enter HOTSPUR, WORCESTER, MORTIMER, *and* GLENDOWER.

MORT. These promises are fair, the parties sure,
And our induction full of prosperous hope.
HOT. Lord Mortimer, and cousin Glendower,
Will you sit down?

SCENE 9
*Interior. Glendower's
Castle. A large
Chamber. Night.*

And uncle Worcester—a plague upon it!   5
I have forgot the map.
GLEND.   No, here it is.
Sit, cousin Percy; sit, good cousin Hotspur,
For by that name as oft as Lancaster
Doth speak of you, his cheek looks pale, and with
A rising sigh he wisheth you in heaven.   10
HOT. And you in hell, as oft as he hears
Owen Glendower spoke of.
GLEND. I cannot blame him: at my nativity
The front of heaven was full of fiery shapes,
Of burning cressets; and at my birth   15
The frame and huge foundation of the earth
Shaked like a coward.
HOT.   Why, so it would have done at the same
season if your mother's cat had but kitten'd, though yourself had
never been born.   20
GLEND. I say the earth did shake when I was born.
HOT. And I say the earth was not of my mind,
If you suppose as fearing you it shook.
GLEND. The heavens were all on fire, the earth did tremble.
HOT. O, then the earth shook to see the heavens on fire,   25
And not in fear of your nativity.
Diseased nature oftentimes breaks forth
In strange eruptions; oft the teeming earth
Is with a kind of colic pinch'd and vex'd
By the imprisoning of unruly wind   30
Within her womb; which, for enlargement striving,
Shakes the old beldam earth, and topples down
Steeples and moss-grown towers.   At your birth,
Our grandam earth, having this distemp'rature,
In passion shook.
GLEND.   Cousin, of many men   35
I do not bear these crossings.   Give me leave
To tell you once again that at my birth
The front of heaven was full of fiery shapes,
The goats ran from the mountains, and the herds
Were strangely clamorous to the frighted fields.   40
These signs have mark'd me extraordinary;
And all the courses of my life do show
I am not in the roll of common men.
Where is he living, clipp'd in with the sea
That chides the banks of England, Scotland, Wales,   45
Which calls me pupil or hath read to me?
And bring him out that is but woman's son
Can trace me in the tedious ways of art
And hold me pace in deep experiments.
HOT. I think there's no man speaks better Welsh.   I'll to dinner.
MORT. Peace, cousin Percy; you will make him mad.
GLEND. I can call spirits from the vasty deep.
HOT. Why, so can I, or so can any man;
But will they come when you do call for them?   55
GLEND. Why, I can teach you, cousin, to command
The devil.

Lines 27–35, 'In passion shook', omitted.

Lines 42–49 omitted.

HOT. And I can teach thee, coz, to shame the devil
    By telling truth : <u>tell truth, and shame the devil</u>.
    If thou have power to raise him, bring him hither,   60
    And I'll be sworn I have power to shame him hence.
    O, while you live, tell truth, and shame the devil !
MORT. Come, come, no more of this unprofitable chat.
GLEND. Three times hath Henry Bolingbroke made head
    Against my power ; thrice from the banks of Wye   65
    And sandy-bottom'd Severn have I sent him
    Bootless home and weather-beaten back.
HOT. Home without boots, and in foul weather too !
    How scapes he agues, in the devil's name ?
GLEND. Come, here is the map ; shall we divide our right   70
    According to our threefold order ta'en ?
MORT. The Archdeacon hath divided it
    Into three limits very equally :
    England, from Trent and Severn hitherto,
    By south and east is to my part assign'd ;   75
    All westward, Wales beyond the Severn shore,
    And all the fertile land within that bound,
    To Owen Glendower ; and, dear coz, to you
    The remnant northward lying off from Trent.
    And our indentures tripartite are drawn ;   80
    Which being sealed interchangeably,
    A business that this night may execute,
    To-morrow, cousin Percy, you and I
    And my good Lord of Worcester will set forth
    To meet your father and the Scottish power,   85
    As is appointed us, at Shrewsbury.
    My father Glendower is not ready yet,
    Nor shall we need his help these fourteen days.
    [*To* GLENDOWER.]   Within that space you may have drawn together
    Your tenants, friends, and neighbouring gentlemen.   90
GLEND. A shorter time shall send me to you, lords ; | Lines 91–95 omitted.
    And in my conduct shall your ladies come, |
    From whom you now must steal and take no leave ; |
    For there will be a world of water shed |
    Upon the parting of your wives and you.   95 |
HOT. Methinks my moiety, north from Burton here,
    In quantity equals not one of yours.
    See how this river comes me cranking in,
    And cuts me from the best of all my land
    A huge half-moon, a monstrous cantle out.   100
    I'll have the current in this place damm'd up,
    And here the smug and silver Trent shall run
    In a new channel, fair and evenly ;
    It shall not wind with such a deep indent
    To rob me of so rich a bottom here.   105
GLEND. Not wind ! It shall, it must ; you see it doth.
MORT. Yea, but
    Mark how he bears his course and runs me up
    With like advantage on the other side,
    Gelding the opposed continent as much   110
    As on the other side it takes from you.

WOR. Yea, but a little charge will trench him here,
    And on this north side win this cape of land,
    And then he runs straight and even.
HOT. I'll have it so ; a little charge will do it.   115
GLEND. I'll not have it alt'red.
HOT.   Will not you ?
GLEND. No, nor you shall not.
HOT.   Who shall say me nay ?
GLEND. Why, that will I.
HOT. Let me not understand you, then ; speak it in Welsh.
GLEND. I can speak English, lord, as well as you,
    For I was train'd up in the English court ;
    Where, being but young, I framed to the harp
    Many an English ditty lovely well,
    And gave the tongue a helpful ornament—   125
    A virtue that was never seen in you.
HOT. Marry,
    And I am glad of it with all my heart !
    I had rather be a kitten and cry mew
    Than one of these same metre ballad-mongers ;   130
    I had rather hear a brazen canstick turn'd,
    Or a dry wheel grate on the axle-tree ;
    And that would set my teeth nothing on edge,
    Nothing so much as mincing poetry.
    'Tis like the forc'd gait of a shuffling nag.   135
GLEND. Come, you shall have Trent turn'd.
HOT. I do not care ; I'll give thrice so much land
    To any well-deserving friend ;
    But in the way of bargain, mark ye me,
    I'll cavil on the ninth part of a hair.   140
    Are the indentures drawn ?   Shall we be gone ?
GLEND. The moon shines fair ; you may away by night ;
    I'll haste the writer, and withal
    Break with your wives of your departure hence.
    I am afraid my daughter will run mad,   145
    So much she doteth on her Mortimer.   [*Exit.*
MORT. Fie, cousin Percy ! how you cross my father !
HOT. I cannot choose. Sometime he angers me
    With telling me of the moldwarp and the ant,
    Of the dreamer Merlin and his prophecies,   150
    And of a dragon and a finless fish,
    A clip-wing'd griffin and a moulten raven,
    A couching lion and a ramping cat,
    And such a deal of skimbie-skamble stuff
    As puts me from my faith. I tell you what :   155
    He held me last night at least nine hours
    In reckoning up the several devils' names
    That were his lackeys. I cried ' hum ' and ' well, go to '
    But mark'd him not a word. O, he is as tedious
    As a tired horse, a railing wife ;   160
    Worse than a smoky house ; I had rather live
    With cheese and garlic in a windmill, far,
    Than feed on cates and have him talk to me
    In any summer house in Christendom.

Lines 150–153
omitted.

According to Holinshed, the division of the kingdom was made by
the conspirators "through a foolish credit given to a vain prophecy"
that Henry was a moldwarp (mole) whose kingdom should be
divided among a wolf, a dragon, and 63 a lion. The
prophecy was attributed to Merlin, and is referred to
in _The Mirror for Magistrates_ (1559).

MORT. In faith, he is a worthy gentleman,   165
    Exceedingly well read, and profited
    In strange concealments ; valiant as a lion,
    And wondrous affable ; and as bountiful
    As mines of India.   Shall I tell you, cousin ?
    He holds your temper in a high respect,   170
    And curbs himself even of his natural scope
    When you come 'cross his humour ; faith, he does.
    I warrant you that man is not alive
    Might so have tempted him as you have done
    Without the taste of danger and reproof ;   175
    But do not use it oft, let me entreat you.
WOR. In faith, my lord, you are too wilful-blame ;
    And since your coming hither have done enough
    To put him quite besides his patience.
    You must needs learn, lord, to amend this fault ;   180
    Though sometimes it show greatness, courage, blood—   Lines 181–189
    And that's the dearest grace it renders you—   omitted.
    Yet oftentimes it doth present harsh rage,
    Defect of manners, want of government,
    Pride, haughtiness, opinion, and disdain ;   185
    The least of which, haunting a nobleman,
    Loseth men's hearts, and leaves behind a stain
    Upon the beauty of all parts besides,
    Beguiling them of commendation.
HOT. Well, I am school'd : good manners be your speed !   190
    Here come our wives, and let us take our leave.

Re-enter GLENDOWER, *with* LADY MORTIMER *and* LADY PERCY.

MORT. This is the deadly spite that angers me :
    My wife can speak no English, I no Welsh.
GLEND. My daughter weeps : she'll not part with you ;
    She'll be a soldier too, she'll to the wars.   195
MORT. Good father, tell her that she and my aunt Percy
    Shall follow in your conduct speedily.
[GLENDOWER *speaks to her in Welsh, and she answers him in the same.*   See A opposite.
GLEND. She is desperate here ; a peevish, self-will'd harlotry, one
    that no persuasion can do good upon.
                           [*The* LADY *speaks in Welsh.*   See B opposite.
MORT. I understand thy looks : that pretty Welsh   200
    Which thou pourest down from these swelling heavens
    I am too perfect in ; and, but for shame,
    In such a parley should I answer thee.
                           [*The* LADY *speaks again in Welsh.*   See C opposite.
    I understand thy kisses, and thou mine,
    And that's a feeling disputation ;   205
    But I will never be a truant, love,
    Till I have learnt thy language ; for thy tongue
    Makes Welsh as sweet as ditties highly penn'd,
    Sung by a fair queen in a summer's bow'r,
    With ravishing division, to her lute.   210
GLEND. Nay, if you melt, then will she run mad.
                           [*The* LADY *speaks again in Welsh.*   See D opposite.
MORT. O, I am ignorance itself in this !

The Welsh dialogue referred to opposite has, with its English translation, been specially written for the BBC television production and is reproduced below.

A GLEND. Fy mhlentyn, bydd di'n amyneddgar dro.
Gweddus yw pryder mawr dy ŵr
Dros dy ddedwyddyd.
Archodd i mi ddywedyd y cei di
A'r fwyn Arglwyddes Persi
Oedi am dymor eto dan fy nawdd.

My child, be patient yet awhile.
Your husband, as is meet, shows great concern
For your correct disposal.
And bids me tell you that together with
The Lady Percy
You must continue under my protection.

LADY MORT. Fy arglwydd, na. Yno y mae fy lle,
Yn ymyl fy rhinweddol gymar byth.
Cans pa le bynnag y bo yntau y byddaf fi.
A thrwy ymrwymiad ein priodasol lw,
A wad i mi ei wely gyda'r nos
Mi ni oddefaf ddim.

Nay, my lord. My place is there
Forever at my noble husband's side.
Wherever he adventures so will I.
And by the bonds of wedlock
I'll not consent to aught which
Shall deny the nightly access to his bed.

B LADY MORT. Onid ei wraig wyf fi? Onid fy arglwydd ef?
Pa le y mae gorffwysfa imi felly
Ond yn ei ymyl?

Am I his wife? And is not he my Lord?
Where other place is now my stay
But with my husband?

C LADY MORT. Fy Arglwydd rhadlon.
Mwy nid tan iau dyletswydd y llefaraf.
Cariad – tyneraf a phrydferthaf nwyd
Yw grym fy ewyllys. Fy arglwydd tyner,
Gyda thi gad i mi fyned.

My gracious Lord.
It is not solely duty bids me speak.
But that most tender passion – love
Now rules my will. And tenderly I plead
Let me go with you. My sweet Lord.

D LADY MORT. Tyred, fy arglwydd ac fe'th hudaf di:
Yma ar wely o frwyn yn ddistaw gorwedd;
Gwrando ddyrïau hen dan nawdd fy mynwes,
I leddfu holl ofalon byd a'i boen.

Come, good my Lord, and I will charm you.
Lie down upon the rushes here and
Cradled in my lap I'll sing your best loved songs
Shall make you soon forget these all ungentle cares.   65

GLEND. She bids you on the wanton rushes lay you down,
And rest your gentle head upon her lap,
And she will sing the song that pleaseth you, 215
And on your eyelids crown the god of sleep,
Charming your blood with pleasing heaviness,
Making such difference 'twixt wake and sleep
As is the difference betwixt day and night
The hour before the heavenly-harness'd team 220
Begins his golden progress in the east.
MORT. With all my heart I'll sit and hear her sing;
By that time will our book, I think, be drawn.
GLEND. Do so;
And those musicians that shall play to you 225
Hang in the air a thousand leagues from hence,
And straight they shall be here; sit, and attend.
HOT. Come, Kate, thou art perfect in lying down. Come, quick,
quick, that I may lay my head in thy lap.
LADY P. Go, ye giddy goose. [The music plays.
HOT. Now I perceive the devil understands Welsh;
And 'tis no marvel he is so humorous.
By'r lady, he is a good musician.
LADY P. Then should you be nothing but musical, for you are
altogether govern'd by humours. Lie still, ye thief, and hear the
lady sing in Welsh. 236
HOT. I had rather hear Lady, my brach, howl in Irish.
LADY P. Wouldst thou have thy head broken?
HOT. No.
LADY P. Then be still. 240
HOT. Neither; 'tis a woman's fault.
LADY P. Now God help thee!
HOT. To the Welsh lady's bed.
LADY P. What's that?
HOT. Peace! she sings. [Here the LADY sings a Welsh song.
HOT. Come, Kate, I'll have your song too.
LADY P. Not mine, in good sooth.
HOT. Not yours, in good sooth! Heart! you swear like a comfit-
maker's wife. 'Not you, in good sooth' and 'As true as I live'
and 'As God shall mend me' and 'As sure as day'. 251
And givest such sarcenet surety for thy oaths
As if thou never walk'st further than Finsbury.
Swear me, Kate, like a lady as thou art,
A good mouth-filling oath; and leave 'in sooth', 255
And such protest of pepper-gingerbread
To velvet-guards and Sunday-citizens.
Come, sing.
LADY P. I will not sing. 259
HOT. 'Tis the next way to turn tailor, or be redbreast teacher. An
the indentures be drawn, I'll away within these two hours; and
so come in when ye will. [Exit.
GLEND. Come, come, Lord Mortimer; you are as slow
As hot Lord Percy is on fire to go.
By this our book is drawn; we'll but seal, 265
And then to horse immediately.
MORT. With all my heart. [Exeunt.

SCENE II. *London.   The palace.*

Enter the KING, *the* PRINCE OF WALES, *and* LORDS.

SCENE 10
*Interior. London. The
Royal Palace. Day.*
KING, PRINCE OF
WALES.
Lines 1–3 omitted.

KING. Lords, give us leave ; the Prince of Wales and I
  Must have some private conference ; but be near at hand,
  For we shall presently have need of you.   [*Exeunt* Lords.
  I know not whether God will have it so,
  For some displeasing service I have done,   5
  That, in his secret doom, out of my blood
  He'll breed revengement and a scourge for me ;
  But thou dost in thy passages of life
  Make me believe that thou art only mark'd
  For the hot vengeance and the rod of heaven   10
  To punish my mistreadings.   Tell me else,
  Could such inordinate and low desires,
  Such poor, such bare, such lewd, such mean attempts,
  Such barren pleasures, rude society,
  As thou art match'd withal and grafted to,   15
  Accompany the greatness of thy blood
  And hold their level with thy princely heart ?
PRINCE. So please your Majesty, I would I could
  Quit all offences with as clear excuse,
  As well as I am doubtless I can purge   20
  Myself of many I am charg'd withal ;
  Yet such extenuation let me beg,
  As, in reproof of many tales devis'd,
  Which oft the ear of greatness needs must hear,
  By smiling pick-thanks and base newsmongers,   25
  I may, for some things true, wherein my youth
  Hath faulty wand'red and irregular,
  Find pardon on my true submission.
KING. God pardon thee !   Yet let me wonder, Harry,
  At thy affections, which do hold a wing   30
  Quite from the flight of all thy ancestors.
  Thy place in council thou hast rudely lost,
  Which by thy younger brother is supplied,
  And art almost an alien to the hearts
  Of all the court and princes of my blood.   35
  The hope and expectation of thy time
  Is ruin'd, and the soul of every man
  Prophetically do forethink thy fall.
  Had I so lavish of my presence been,
  So common-hackney'd in the eyes of men,   40
  So stale and cheap to vulgar company,
  Opinion, that did help me to the crown,
  Had still kept loyal to possession
  And left me in reputeless banishment
  A fellow of no mark nor likelihood.   45
  By being seldom seen, I could not stir
  But, like a comet, I was wond'red at ;
  That men would tell their children ' This is he ' ;
  Others would say ' Where, which is Bolingbroke ? '
  And then I stole all courtesy from heaven,   50
  And dress'd myself in such humility

That I did pluck allegiance from men's hearts,
Loud shouts and salutations from their mouths,
Even in the presence of the crowned King.
Thus did I keep my person fresh and new,   55
My presence, like a robe pontifical,
Ne'er seen but wond'red at, and so my state,
Seldom but sumptuous, show'd like a feast
And won by rareness such solemnity.
The skipping King, he ambled up and down   60
With shallow jesters and rash bavin wits,
Soon kindled and soon burnt; carded his state,
Mingled his royalty with cap'ring fools;
Had his great name profaned with their scorns,
And gave his countenance, against his name,   65
To laugh at gibing boys and stand the push
Of every beardless vain comparative;
Grew a companion to the common streets,
Enfeoff'd himself to popularity;
That, being daily swallowed by men's eyes,   70
They surfeited with honey and began
To loathe the taste of sweetness, whereof a little
More than a little is by much too much.
So, when he had occasion to be seen,
He was but as the cuckoo is in June,   75
Heard, not regarded, seen, but with such eyes
As, sick and blunted with community,
Afford no extraordinary gaze,
Such as is bent on sun-like majesty
When it shines seldom in admiring eyes;   80
But rather drowz'd and hung their eyelids down,
Slept in his face, and rend'red such aspect
As cloudy men use to their adversaries,
Being with his presence glutted, gorg'd, and full.
And in that very line, Harry, standest thou;   85
For thou hast lost thy princely privilege
With vile participation. Not an eye
But is aweary of thy common sight,
Save mine, which hath desir'd to see thee more;
Which now doth that I would not have it do—   90
Make blind itself with foolish tenderness.
PRINCE. I shall hereafter, my thrice-gracious lord,
  Be more myself.
KING.   For all the world
As thou art to this hour was Richard then
When I from France set foot at Ravenspurgh;
And even as I was then is Percy now.   95
Now, by my sceptre and my soul to boot,
He hath more worthy interest to the state
Than thou the shadow of succession;
For of no right, nor colour like to right,   100
He doth fill fields with harness in the realm;
Turns head against the lion's armed jaws;
And, being no more in debt to years than thou,
Leads ancient lords and reverend bishops on

To bloody battles and to bruising arms.   105
What never-dying honour hath he got
Against renowned Douglas ! whose high deeds,
Whose hot incursions, and great name in arms,
Holds from all soldiers chief majority
And military title capital   110
Through all the kingdoms that acknowledge Christ.
Thrice hath this Hotspur, Mars in swathling clothes, | Lines 112–117
This infant warrior, in his enterprises | omitted.
Discomfited great Douglas ; ta'en him once,
Enlarged him and made a friend of him,   115
To fill the mouth of deep defiance up
And shake the peace and safety of our throne.
And what say you to this ?   Percy, Northumberland,
The Archbishop's Grace of York, Douglas, Mortimer,
Capitulate against us and are up.   120
But wherefore do I tell these news to thee ?
Why, Harry, do I tell thee of my foes,
Which art my nearest and dearest enemy ?
Thou that art like enough, through vassal fear,
Base inclination, and the start of spleen,   125
To fight against me under Percy's pay,
To dog his heels, and curtsy at his frowns,
To show how much thou art degenerate.
PRINCE. Do not think so ; you shall not find it so ;
And God forgive them that so much have sway'd   130
Your Majesty's good thoughts away from me !
I will redeem all this on Percy's head,
And in the closing of some glorious day
Be bold to tell you that I am your son,
When I will wear a garment all of blood,   135
And stain my favours in a bloody mask,
Which, wash'd away, shall scour my shame with it ;
And that shall be the day, whene'er it lights,
That this same child of honour and renown,
This gallant Hotspur, this all-praised knight,   140
And your unthought-of Harry chance to meet.
For every honour sitting on his helm,
Would they were multitudes, and on my head
My shames redoubled !   For the time will come
That I shall make this northern youth exchange   145
His glorious deeds for my indignities.
Percy is but my factor, good my lord,
To engross up glorious deeds on my behalf ;
And I will call him to so strict account
That he shall render every glory up,   150
Yea, even the slightest worship of his time,
Or I will tear the reckoning from his heart.
This, in the name of God, I promise here ;
The which if He be pleas'd I shall perform,
I do beseech your Majesty may salve   155
The long-grown wounds of my intemperature.
If not, the end of life cancels all bands ;
And I will die a hundred thousand deaths

Ere break the smallest parcel of this vow.
KING. A hundred thousand rebels die in this :   160
Thou shalt have charge and sovereign trust herein.

Enter SIR WALTER BLUNT.

How now, good Blunt ! Thy looks are full of speed.
BLUNT. So hath the business that I come to speak of.
Lord Mortimer of Scotland hath sent word
That Douglas and the English rebels met   165
The eleventh of this month at Shrewsbury.
A mighty and a fearful head they are,
If promises be kept on every hand,
As ever off'red foul play in a state.
KING. The Earl of Westmoreland set forth to-day,   170
With him my son, Lord John of Lancaster ;
For this advertisement is five days old.
On Wednesday next, Harry, you shall set forward ;
On Thursday we ourselves will march. Our meeting
Is Bridgenorth. And, Harry, you shall march   175
Through Gloucestershire ; by which account,
Our business valued, some twelve days hence
Our general forces at Bridgenorth shall meet.
Our hands are full of business. Let's away.
Advantage feeds him fat while men delay.   [*Exeunt.*

Lines 162–180
omitted.

SCENE III. *Eastcheap. The Boar's Head Tavern.*

Enter FALSTAFF *and* BARDOLPH.

FAL. Bardolph, am I not fall'n away vilely since this last action ?
Do I not bate ? Do I not dwindle ? Why, my skin hangs
about me like an old lady's loose gown ; I am withered like an
old apple-john. Well, I'll repent, and that suddenly, while I am
in some liking ; I shall be out of heart shortly, and then I shall
have no strength to repent. An I have not forgotten what the
inside of a church is made of, I am a peppercorn, a brewer's
horse. The inside of a church ! Company, villainous company,
hath been the spoil of me.   10
BARD. Sir John, you are so fretful you cannot live long.
FAL. Why, there is it ; come, sing me a bawdy song, make me
merry. I was as virtuously given as a gentleman need to be ;
virtuous enough : swore little, dic'd not above seven times a
week, went to a bawdy-house not above once in a quarter—of
an hour, paid money that I borrowed—three or four times, lived
well, and in good compass ; and now I live out of all order, out
of all compass.   20
BARD. Why, you are so fat, Sir John, that you must needs be out
of all compass—out of all reasonable compass, Sir John.
FAL. Do thou amend thy face, and I'll amend my life. Thou art
our admiral, thou bearest the lantern in the poop, but 'tis in the
nose of thee ; thou art the Knight of the Burning Lamp.   27
BARD. Why, Sir John, my face does you no harm.
FAL. No, I'll be sworn ; I make as good use of it as many a man
doth of a death's head or a memento mori : I never see thy face

SCENE II
Interior. Eastcheap.
The Boar's Head
Tavern. Day.

but I think upon hell-fire, and Dives that lived in purple ; for
there he is in his robes, burning, burning. If thou wert any
way given to virtue, I would swear by thy face : my oath should
be ' By this fire, that's God's angel '. But thou art altogether
given over, and wert indeed, but for the light in thy face, the
son of utter darkness. When thou ran'st up Gadshill in the
night to catch my horse, if I did not think thou hadst been an
ignis fatuus or a ball of wildfire, there's no purchase in money.
O, thou art a perpetual triumph, an everlasting bonfire light !
Thou hast saved me a thousand marks in links and torches,
walking with thee in the night betwixt tavern and tavern ; but
the sack that thou hast drunk me would have bought me lights
as good cheap at the dearest chandler's in Europe. I have
maintained that salamander of yours with fire any time this two
and thirty years ; God reward me for it !   47
BARD. 'Sblood, I would my face were in your belly !
FAL. God-a-mercy ! so should I be sure to be heart-burnt.

Enter Hostess.

How now, Dame Partlet the hen ! Have you inquir'd yet who
pick'd my pocket ?
HOST. Why, Sir John, what do you think, Sir John ? Do you think
I keep thieves in my house ? I have search'd, I have inquired,
so has my husband, man by man, boy by boy, servant by servant.
The tithe of a hair was never lost in my house before.   57
FAL. Ye lie, hostess : Bardolph was shav'd and lost many a hair,
and I'll be sworn my pocket was pick'd. Go to, you are a woman,
go.   60
HOST. Who, I ? No, I defy thee. God's light, I was never call'd
so in mine own house before.
FAL. Go to, I know you well enough.
HOST. No, Sir John, you do not know me, Sir John. I know you,
Sir John : you owe me money, Sir John ; and now you pick a
quarrel to beguile me of it. I bought you a dozen of shirts to
your back.   67
FAL. Dowlas, filthy dowlas ! I have given them away to bakers'
wives ; they have made bolters of them.
HOST. Now, as I am a true woman, holland of eight shillings an ell.
You owe money here besides, Sir John, for your diet and by-
drinkings, and money lent you, four and twenty pound.
FAL. He had his part of it ; let him pay.
HOST. He ? Alas, he is poor ; he hath nothing.   75
FAL. How ! poor ? Look upon his face : what call you rich ? Let
them coin his nose, let them coin his cheeks. I'll not pay a
denier. What, will you make a younker of me ? Shall I not
take mine ease in mine inn but I shall have my pocket pick'd ?
I have lost a seal-ring of my grandfather's worth forty mark.
HOST. O Jesu, I have heard the Prince tell him, I know not how oft,
that that ring was copper !
FAL. How ! the Prince is a Jack, a sneak-cup. 'Sblood, an he were
here, I would cudgel him like a dog if he would say so.   86

Enter the PRINCE *marching, with* PETO ; *and* FALSTAFF *meets him,
playing upon his truncheon like a fife.*

'If thou wert . . .
purchase in money'
omitted.

The name of the hen
in the famous story
of the Cock and the
fox ; cf. Chaucer's
Nonnes Preestes
Tale.

'so has my husband'
omitted.

For 'PETO' read
'POINS'.

Brenda Bruce as Mistress Quickly

FAL. How now, lad! Is the wind in that door, i' faith? Must we
all march?
BARD. Yea, two and two, Newgate fashion.
HOST. My lord, I pray you hear me.   90
PRINCE. What say'st thou, Mistress Quickly? How doth thy hus-   Lines 91–93 omitted.
band? I love him well; he is an honest man.
HOST. Good my lord, hear me.
FAL. Prithee, let her alone, and list to me.
PRINCE. What say'st thou, Jack?
FAL. The other night I fell asleep here behind the arras and had
my pocket pick'd; this house is turn'd bawdy-house; they pick
pockets.
PRINCE. What didst thou lose, Jack?   100
FAL. Wilt thou believe me, Hal? Three or four bonds of forty
pound a-piece and a seal-ring of my grandfather's.
PRINCE. A trifle, some eight-penny matter.
HOST. So I told him, my lord; and I said I heard your Grace say
so; and, my lord, he speaks most vilely of you, like a foul-
mouth'd man as he is, and said he would cudgel you.
PRINCE. What! he did not?
HOST. There's neither faith, truth, nor womanhood, in me else. 111
FAL. There's no more faith in thee than in a stewed prune; nor no   'nor no more . . .
more truth in thee than in a drawn fox; and for womanhood,   ward to thee'
Maid Marian may be the deputy's wife of the ward to thee.   omitted.
Go, you thing, go.
HOST. Say, what thing? what thing?
FAL. What thing! Why, a thing to thank God on.
HOST. I am no thing to thank God on, I would thou shouldst know   'I would . . . man's
it; I am an honest man's wife; and setting thy knighthood   wife' omitted.
aside, thou art a knave to call me so.   121
FAL. Setting thy womanhood aside, thou art a beast to say otherwise.
HOST. Say, what beast, thou knave, thou?
FAL. What beast! Why, an otter.
PRINCE. An otter, Sir John! Why an otter?
FAL. Why, she's neither fish nor flesh: a man knows not where to
have her.   128
HOST. Thou art an unjust man in saying so: thou or any man knows
where to have me, thou knave, thou!
PRINCE. Thou say'st true, hostess; and he slanders thee most grossly.
HOST. So he doth you, my lord; and said this other day you ought   Lines 133–154, 'So
him a thousand pound.   134   he doth you . . . and
PRINCE. Sirrah, do I owe you a thousand pound?   midriff', omitted.
FAL. A thousand pound, Hal! A million.
Thy love is worth a million: thou owest me thy love.
HOST. Nay, my lord, he call'd you Jack, and said he would cudgel you.
FAL. Did I, Bardolph?   140
BARD. Indeed, Sir John, you said so.
FAL. Yea, if he said my ring was copper.
PRINCE. I say 'tis copper. Darest thou be as good as thy word now?
FAL. Why, Hal, thou knowest, as thou art but man, I dare; but
as thou art prince, I fear thee as I fear the roaring of the lion's
whelp.
PRINCE. And why not as the lion?
FAL. The King himself is to be feared as the lion. Dost thou think

I'll fear thee as I fear thy father? Nay, an I do, I pray God
my girdle break.   151
PRINCE. O, if it should, how would thy guts fall about thy knees!
But, sirrah, there's no room for faith, truth, nor honesty, in this
bosom of thine—it is all fill'd up with guts and midriff. Charge
an honest woman with picking thy pocket! Why, thou whoreson,
impudent, emboss'd rascal, if there were anything in thy pocket
but tavern-reckonings, memorandums of bawdy-houses, and one
poor penny-worth of sugar-candy to make thee long-winded—
if thy pocket were enrich'd with any other injuries but these,
I am a villain. And yet you will stand to it, you will not pocket-
up wrong. Art thou not ashamed?   163
FAL. Dost thou hear, Hal? Thou knowest in the state of innocency
Adam fell; and what should poor Jack Falstaff do in the days
of villainy? Thou seest I have more flesh than another man,
and therefore more frailty. You confess, then, you pick'd my
pocket?
PRINCE. It appears so by the story.   169
FAL. Hostess, I forgive thee. Go make ready breakfast, love thy
husband, look to thy servants, cherish thy guests. Thou shalt
find me tractable to any honest reason. Thou seest I am pacified
still. Nay, prithee, be gone. [Exit Hostess.] Now, Hal, to the
news at court: for the robbery, lad, how is that answered?   175
PRINCE. O, my sweet beef, I must still be good angel to thee: the
money is paid back again.
FAL. O, I do not like that paying back; 'tis a double labour.
PRINCE. I am good friends with my father, and may do anything.
FAL. Rob me the exchequer the first thing thou doest, and do it with
unwash'd hands too.
BARD. Do, my lord.
PRINCE. I have procured thee, Jack, a charge of foot.   184
FAL. I would it had been of horse. Where shall I find one that can
steal well? O for a fine thief, of the age of two and twenty or
thereabouts! I am heinously unprovided. Well, God be
thanked for these rebels—they offend none but the virtuous; I
laud them, I praise them.   191
PRINCE. Bardolph!
BARD. My lord?
PRINCE. Go bear this letter to Lord John of Lancaster,
To my brother John; this to my Lord of Westmoreland.
                                                    [Exit BARDOLPH.
Go, Peto, to horse, to horse; for thou and I
Have thirty miles to ride yet ere dinner-time.   [Exit PETO.
Jack, meet me to-morrow in the Temple Hall
At two o'clock in the afternoon;
There shalt thou know thy charge, and there receive   200
Money and order for their furniture.
The land is burning; Percy stands on high;
And either we or they must lower lie.   [Exit.
FAL. Rare words! brave world! Hostess, my breakfast, come!
O, I could wish this tavern were my drum!   [Exit.

Lines 133–154, 'So
he doth you . . . and
midriff', omitted.

'And yet you will . . .
more frailty' omitted.

'love thy husband'
omitted.
'Thou shalt . . .
pacified still'
omitted.

Lines 185–191
omitted.

Lines 196–197
omitted.

ACT FOUR

SCENE I. *The rebel camp near Shrewsbury.*

Enter HOTSPUR, WORCESTER, *and* DOUGLAS.

SCENE 12
*Interior. A Tent in the
Rebel Camp. Day.*

HOT. Well said, my noble Scot. If speaking truth
In this fine age were not thought flattery,
Such attribution should the Douglas have
As not a soldier of this season's stamp
Should go so general current through the world.   5
By God, I cannot flatter ; I do defy
The tongues of soothers ; but a braver place
In my heart's love hath no man than yourself.
Nay, task me to my word ; approve me, lord.
DOUG. Thou art the king of honour :   10
No man so potent breathes upon the ground
But I will beard him.
HOT.   Do so, and 'tis well.

Enter a Messenger *with letters.*

What letters hast thou there ?—I can but thank you.
MESS. These letters come from your father.
HOT. Letters from him ! Why comes he not himself ?   15
MESS. He cannot come, my lord, he is grievous sick.
HOT. Zounds ! how has he the leisure to be sick
In such a justling time ? Who leads his power ?
Under whose government come they along ?
MESS. His letters bears his mind, not I, my lord.   20
WOR. I prithee tell me, doth he keep his bed ?
MESS. He did, my lord, four days ere I set forth ;
And at the time of my departure thence
He was much fear'd by his physicians.
WOR. I would the state of time had first been whole   25
Ere he by sickness had been visited :
His health was never better worth than now.
HOT. Sick now ! droop now ! This sickness doth infect
The very life-blood of our enterprise ;
'Tis catching hither, even to our camp.   30
He writes me here that inward sickness—
And that his friends by deputation could not
So soon be drawn ; nor did he think it meet
To lay so dangerous and dear a trust
On any soul remov'd, but on his own.   35
Yet doth he give us bold advertisement
That with our small conjunction we should on,
To see how fortune is dispos'd to us ;
For, as he writes, there is no quailing now,
Because the King is certainly possess'd   40
Of all our purposes. What say you to it ?
WOR. Your father's sickness is a maim to us.
HOT. A perilous gash, a very limb lopp'd off.
And yet, in faith, it is not. His present want
Seems more than we shall find it. Were it good   45

Lines 44, 'His
present want', to 75
omitted.

To set the exact wealth of all our states
All at one cast ?   To set so rich a main
On the nice hazard of one doubtful hour ?
It were not good ; for therein should we read
The very bottom and the soul of hope,   50
The very list, the very utmost bound
Of all our fortunes.
DOUG.   Faith, and so we should;
Where now remains a sweet reversion,
We may boldly spend upon the hope of what
Is to come in.   55
A comfort of retirement lives in this.
HOT. A rendezvous, a home to fly unto,
If that the devil and mischance look big
Upon the maidenhead of our affairs.
WOR. But yet I would your father had been here.   60
The quality and hair of our attempt
Brooks no division.   It will be thought
By some, that know not why he is away,
That wisdom, loyalty, and mere dislike
Of our proceedings, kept the earl from hence ;   65
And think how such an apprehension
May turn the tide of fearful faction
And breed a kind of question in our cause ;
For well you know we of the off'ring side
Must keep aloof from strict arbitrement,   70
And stop all sight-holes, every loop from whence
The eye of reason may pry in upon us.
This absence of your father's draws a curtain
That shows the ignorant a kind of fear
Before not dreamt of.
HOT.   You strain too far.   75
I rather of his absence make this use :
It lends a lustre and more great opinion,
A larger dare to our great enterprise,
Than if the earl were here ; for men must think,
If we, without his help, can make a head   80
To push against a kingdom, with his help
We shall o'erturn it topsy-turvy down.
Yet all goes well, yet all our joints are whole.
DOUG. As heart can think ; there is not such a word
Spoke of in Scotland as this term of fear.   85

Enter SIR RICHARD VERNON.

HOT. My cousin Vernon ! welcome, by my soul.
VER. Pray God my news be worth a welcome, lord.
The Earl of Westmoreland, seven thousand strong,
Is marching hitherwards ; with him Prince John.
HOT. No harm ; what more ?
VER.   And further, I have learn'd 90
The King himself in person is set forth,
Or hitherwards intended speedily,
With strong and mighty preparation.
HOT. He shall be welcome too.   Where is his son,

Lines 44–75, 'His
present want . . .
You strain too far',
omitted.

The nimble-footed madcap Prince of Wales,   95
And his comrades that daff'd the world aside
And bid it pass ?
VER.   All furnish'd, all in arms ;
All plum'd like estridges, that with the wind
Bated like eagles having lately bath'd ;
Glittering in golden coats, like images ;   100
As full of spirit as the month of May
And gorgeous as the sun at midsummer ;
Wanton as youthful goats, wild as young bulls.
I saw young Harry with his beaver on,
His cushes on his thighs, gallantly arm'd,   105
Rise from the ground like feathered Mercury,
And vaulted with such ease into his seat
As if an angel dropp'd down from the clouds
To turn and wind a fiery Pegasus,
And witch the world with noble horsemanship.   110
HOT. No more, no more ; worse than the sun in March,
This praise doth nourish agues.   Let them come.
They come like sacrifices in their trim,
And to the fire-ey'd maid of smoky war   *Bellona, goddess of war*
All hot and bleeding will we offer them.   115
The mailed Mars shall on his altar sit
Up to the ears in blood.   I am on fire
To hear this rich reprisa₁ is so nigh
And yet not ours.   Come, let me taste my horse,
Who is to bear me like a thunderbolt   120
Against the bosom of the Prince of Wales.
Harry to Harry shall, hot horse to horse,
Meet, and ne'er part till one drop down a corse.
O that Glendower were come !
VER.   There is more news.
I learn'd in Worcester, as I rode along,   125
He cannot draw his power this fourteen days.
DOUG. That's the worst tidings that I hear of yet.
WOR. Ay, by my faith, that bears a frosty sound.
HOT. What may the King's whole battle reach unto ?
VER. To thirty thousand.
HOT.   Forty let it be :   130
My father and Glendower being both away,
The powers of us may serve so great a day.
Come, let us take a muster speedily.
Doomsday is near ; die all, die merrily.
DOUG. Talk not of dying ; I am out of fear   135
Of death or death's hand for this one half year.   [Exeunt.

           SCENE II.   *A public road near Coventry.*

              Enter FALSTAFF *and* BARDOLPH.

FAL. Bardolph, get thee before to Coventry ; fill me a bottle of sack.
   Our soldiers shall march through ; we'll to Sutton Co'fil' to-night.
BARD. Will you give me money, Captain ?
FAL. Lay out, lay out.   5
BARD. This bottle makes an angel.

SCENE 13
Exterior. A Country
Road near Coventry.
Day.
Line 8, 'Bid my
lieutenant Peto meet
me at town's end',
spoken here.

FAL. An if it do, take it for thy labour; and if it make twenty, take
them all; I'll answer the coinage. Bid my lieutenant Peto meet | Transposed above.
me at town's end.
BARD. I will, Captain; farewell.   [*Exit.*
FAL. If I be not ashamed of my soldiers, I am a sous'd gurnet. I
have misused the King's press damnably. I have got, in exchange
of a hundred and fifty soldiers, three hundred and odd pounds.
I press me none but good householders, yeomen's sons; inquire
me out contracted bachelors, such as had been ask'd twice on
the banns; such a commodity of warm slaves as had as lief hear
the devil as a drum; such as fear the report of a caliver worse
than a struck fowl or a hurt wild-duck. I press'd me none but
such toasts-and-butter, with hearts in their bellies no bigger than
pins' heads, and they have bought out their services; and now
my whole charge consists of ancients, corporals, lieutenants, | 'ancients, corporals
gentlemen of companies—slaves as ragged as Lazarus in the | . . . never soldiers,
painted cloth, where the Glutton's dogs licked his sores; and | but' omitted.
such as indeed were never soldiers, but discarded unjust serving-
men, younger sons to younger brothers, revolted tapsters, and
ostlers trade-fall'n; the cankers of a calm world and a long
peace; ten times more dishonourable ragged than an old-fac'd
ancient. And such have I, to fill up the rooms of them as have
bought out their services, that you would think that I had a
hundred and fifty tattered Prodigals lately come from swine-   Luke 15: 15-16
keeping, from eating draff and husks. A mad fellow met me on
the way, and told me I had unloaded all the gibbets and press'd
the dead bodies. No eye hath seen such scarecrows. I'll not
march through Coventry with them, that's flat. Nay, and the | 'Nay, and the villains
villains march wide betwixt the legs, as if they had gyves on; | . . . on every hedge'
for indeed I had the most of them out of prison. There's not | omitted.
a shirt and a half in all my company; and the half shirt is two
napkins tack'd together and thrown over the shoulders like a
herald's coat without sleeves; and the shirt, to say the truth,
stol'n from my host at Saint Albans, or the red-nose innkeeper
of Daventry. But that's all one; they'll find linen enough on
every hedge.   46

Enter the PRINCE OF WALES *and* WESTMORELAND.

PRINCE. How now, blown Jack! how now, quilt!
FAL. What, Hal! how now, mad wag! What a devil dost thou in
Warwickshire? My good Lord of Westmoreland, I cry you
mercy; I thought your honour had already been at Shrewsbury.
WEST. Faith, Sir John, 'tis more than time that I were there, and
you too; but my powers are there already. The King, I can
tell you, looks for us all; we must away all night.   55
FAL. Tut, never fear me; I am as vigilant as a cat to steal cream.
PRINCE. I think, to steal cream indeed; for thy theft hath already
made thee butter. But tell me, Jack, whose fellows are these
that come after?   60 | 'that come after'
FAL. Mine, Hal, mine. | omitted.
PRINCE. I did never see such pitiful rascals.
FAL. Tut, tut; good enough to toss; food for powder, food for
powder; they'll fill a pit as well as better: tush, man, mortal
men, mortal men.   65

WEST. Ay, but, Sir John, methinks they are exceeding poor and bare—
    too beggarly.
FAL. Faith, for their poverty, I know not where they had that ; and
    for their bareness, I am sure they never learn'd that of me.
PRINCE. No, I'll be sworn ; unless you call three fingers in the ribs
    bare. But, sirrah, make haste ; Percy is already in the field.
                                                        [*Exit.*
FAL. What, is the King encamp'd ?
WEST. He is, Sir John : I fear we shall stay too long.   [*Exit.* 76
FAL. Well,
    To the latter end of a fray and the beginning of a feast
    Fits a dull fighter and a keen guest.   [*Exit.*

          SCENE III.   *The rebel camp near Shrewsbury.*

     Enter HOTSPUR, WORCESTER, DOUGLAS, *and* VERNON.

HOT. We'll fight with him to-night.
WOR.   It may not be.
DOUG. You give him, then, advantage.
VER.   Not a whit.
HOT. Why say you so ? looks he not for supply ?
VER. So do we.
HOT. His is certain, ours is doubtful.
WOR. Good cousin, be advis'd, stir not to-night.   5
VER. Do not, my lord.
DOUG.   You do not counsel well ;
    You speak it out of fear and cold heart.
VER. Do me no slander, Douglas ; by my life,
    And I dare well maintain it with my life,
    If well-respected honour bid me on,   10
    I hold as little counsel with weak fear
    As you, my lord, or any Scot that this day lives ;
    Let it be seen to-morrow in the battle
    Which of us fears.
DOUG.   Yea, or to-night.
VER.   Content.
HOT. To-night, say I.   15
VER. Come, come, it may not be. I wonder much,
    Being men of such great leading as you are,
    That you foresee not what impediments
    Drag back our expedition : certain horse
    Of my cousin Vernon's are not yet come up ;   20
    Your uncle Worcester's horse came but to-day ;
    And now their pride and mettle is asleep,
    Their courage with hard labour tame and dull,
    That not a horse is half the half of himself.   25
HOT. So are the horses of the enemy
    In general, journey-bated and brought low ;
    The better part of ours are full of rest.
WOR. The number of the King exceedeth ours.
    For God's sake, cousin, stay till all come in.
                [*The trumpet sounds a parley.*

     Enter SIR WALTER BLUNT.

                                       SCENE 14
                                       Exterior. The Rebel
                                       Camp. Night.

BLUNT. I come with gracious offers from the King,   30
  If you vouchsafe me hearing and respect.
HOT. Welcome, Sir Walter Blunt; and would to God
  You were of our determination!
  Some of us love you well; and even those some
  Envy your great deservings and good name,   35
  Because you are not of our quality,
  But stand against us like an enemy.
BLUNT. And God defend but still I should stand so,
  So long as out of limit and true rule
  You stand against anointed majesty!   40
  But, to my charge. The King hath sent to know
  The nature of your griefs; and whereupon
  You conjure from the breast of civil peace
  Such bold hostility, teaching his duteous land
  Audacious cruelty. If that the King   45
  Have any way your good deserts forgot,
  Which he confesseth to be manifold,
  He bids you name your griefs, and with all speed
  You shall have your desires with interest,
  And pardon absolute for yourself and these   50
  Herein misled by your suggestion.
HOT. The King is kind; and well we know the King
  Knows at what time to promise, when to pay.
  My father and my uncle and myself
  Did give him that same royalty he wears;   55
  And when he was not six and twenty strong,
  Sick in the world's regard, wretched and low,
  A poor unminded outlaw sneaking home,
  My father gave him welcome to the shore;
  And when he heard him swear and vow to God   60
  He came but to be Duke of Lancaster,
  To sue his livery and beg his peace,
  With tears of innocency and terms of zeal,
  My father, in kind heart and pity mov'd,
  Swore him assistance, and perform'd it too.   65
  Now when the lords and barons of the realm
  Perceiv'd Northumberland did lean to him,
  The more and less came in with cap and knee;
  Met him in boroughs, cities, villages;
  Attended him on bridges, stood in lanes,   70
  Laid gifts before him, proffer'd him their oaths,
  Gave him their heirs as pages, followed him
  Even at the heels in golden multitudes.
  He presently—as greatness knows itself—
  Steps me a little higher than his vow   75
  Made to my father, while his blood was poor,
  Upon the naked shore at Ravenspurgh;
  And now, forsooth, takes on him to reform
  Some certain edicts, and some strait decrees
  That lie too heavy on the commonwealth;   80
  Cries out upon abuses, seems to weep
  Over his country's wrongs; and by this face,
  This seeming brow of justice, did he win

The hearts of all that he did angle for ;
Proceeded further : cut me off the heads   85
Of all the favourites that the absent King
In deputation left behind him here,
When he was personal in the Irish war.
BLUNT. Tut, I came not to hear this.
HOT.   Then to the point.
    In short time after, he depos'd the King ;   90
    Soon after that depriv'd him of his life ;
    And in the neck of that, task'd the whole state ;
    To make that worse, suff'red his kinsman March—   For 'March' read
    Who is, if every owner were well plac'd,   'Mortimer'.
    Indeed his king—to be engag'd in Wales,   95
    There without ransom to lie forfeited ;
    Disgrac'd me in my happy victories ;
    Sought to entrap me by intelligence ;
    Rated mine uncle from the council-board ;
    In rage dismiss'd my father from the court ;   100
    Broke oath on oath, committed wrong on wrong ;
    And in conclusion drove us to seek out
    This head of safety, and withal to pry
    Into his title, the which we find
    Too indirect for long continuance.   105
BLUNT. Shall I return this answer to the King ?
HOT. Not so, Sir Walter ; we'll withdraw awhile.
    Go to the King ; and let there be impawn'd
    Some surety for a safe return again,
    And in the morning early shall mine uncle   110
    Bring him our purposes. And so, farewell.*   See below.
BLUNT.   Pray God you do.   [Exeunt.

SCENE IV.   York.   The Archbishop's palace.   SCENE 15
                                                      Interior. York.
Enter the ARCHBISHOP OF YORK, and SIR MICHAEL.   A Room in the
                                                      Archbishop's Palace.
ARCH. Hie, good Sir Michael ; bear this sealed brief Night.
    With winged haste to the Lord Marshal ;
    This to my cousin Scroop ; and all the rest
    To whom they are directed.   If you knew
    How much they do import, you would make haste.   5
SIR M. My good lord,
    I guess their tenour.
ARCH.   Like enough you do.
    To-morrow, good Sir Michael, is a day
    Wherein the fortune of ten thousand men
    Must bide the touch ; for, sir, at Shrewsbury,   10
    As I am truly given to understand,
    The King with mighty and quick-raised power
    Meets with Lord Harry ; and I fear, Sir Michael,
    What with the sickness of Northumberland,
    Whose power was in the first proportion,   15
    And what with Owen Glendower's absence thence,
    Who with them was a rated sinew too

* After line 111 two lines have been omitted:
BLUNT. I would yould accept of grace and love.
HOT. And may be so we shall.

And comes not in, o'errul'd by prophecies,
I fear the power of Percy is too weak
To wage an instant trial with the King.   20
SIR M. Why, my good lord, you need not fear ;
There is Douglas and Lord Mortimer.
ARCH. No, Mortimer is not there.
SIR M. But there is Mordake, Vernon, Lord Harry Percy,
And there is my Lord of Worcester, and a head   25
Of gallant warriors, noble gentlemen.
ARCH. And so there is ; but yet the King hath drawn
The special head of all the land together :
The Prince of Wales, Lord John of Lancaster,
The noble Westmoreland, and warlike Blunt ;   30
And many moe corrivals and dear men
Of estimation and command in arms.
SIR M. Doubt not, my lord, they shall be well oppos'd.
ARCH. I hope no less, yet needful 'tis to fear ;
And, to prevent the worst, Sir Michael, speed ;   35
For if Lord Percy thrive not, ere the King
Dismiss his power, he means to visit us—
For he hath heard of our confederacy—
And 'tis but wisdom to make strong against him ;
Therefore make haste.   I must go write again   40
To other friends ; and so farewell, Sir Michael.
                                        [*Exeunt severally.*

| Lines 21–32 omitted. |

ACT FIVE

SCENE I.   *The KING's camp near Shrewsbury.*

Enter the KING, *the* PRINCE OF WALES, PRINCE JOHN OF LANCASTER,
SIR WALTER BLUNT, *and* SIR JOHN FALSTAFF.

SCENE 16
Exterior. The King's Camp near Shrewsbury. Dawn.

KING. How bloodily the sun begins to peer
Above yon busky hill !   The day looks pale
At his distemp'rature.
PRINCE.   The southern wind
Doth play the trumpet to his purposes,
And by his hollow whistling in the leaves   5
Foretells a tempest and a blust'ring day.
KING. Then with the losers let it sympathize,
For nothing can seem foul to those that win. [*The trumpet sounds.*

Enter WORCESTER *and* VERNON.

How now, my Lord of Worcester !   'Tis not well
That you and I should meet upon such terms   10
As now we meet.   You have deceiv'd our trust,
And made us doff our easy robes of peace
To crush our old limbs in ungentle steel ;
This is not well, my lord, this is not well.
What say you to it ?   Will you again unknit   15
This churlish knot of all-abhorred war,
And move in that obedient orb again
Where you did give a fair and natural light,
And be no more an exhal'd meteor,

A prodigy of fear, and a portent   20
Of broached mischief to the unborn times?
WOR. Hear me, my liege:
For mine own part, I could be well content
To entertain the lag-end of my life
With quiet hours; for I protest   25
I have not sought the day of this dislike.
KING. You have not sought it! How comes it then?
FAL. Rebellion lay in his way, and he found it.
PRINCE. Peace, chewet, peace!
WOR. It pleas'd your Majesty to turn your looks   30
Of favour from myself and all our house;
And yet I must remember you, my lord,
We were the first and dearest of your friends.
For you my staff of office did I break
In Richard's time, and posted day and night   35
To meet you on the way and kiss your hand,
When yet you were in place and in account
Nothing so strong and fortunate as I.
It was myself, my brother, and his son,
That brought you home, and boldly did outdare   40
The dangers of the time. You swore to us—
And you did swear that oath at Doncaster—
That you did nothing purpose 'gainst the state,
Nor claim no further than your new-fall'n right,
The seat of Gaunt, dukedom of Lancaster;   45
To this we swore our aid. But in short space
It rain'd down fortune show'ring on your head;
And such a flood of greatness fell on you,
What with our help, what with the absent King,
What with the injuries of a wanton time,   50
The seeming sufferances that you had borne,
And the contrarious winds that held the King
So long in his unlucky Irish wars
That all in England did repute him dead;
And from this swarm of fair advantages   55
You took occasion to be quickly woo'd
To gripe the general sway into your hand;
Forgot your oath to us at Doncaster;
And being fed by us you us'd us so
As that ungentle gull, the cuckoo's bird,   60
Useth the sparrow—did oppress our nest,
Grew by our feeding to so great a bulk
That even our love durst not come near your sight
For fear of swallowing; but with nimble wing
We were enforc'd, for safety sake, to fly   65
Out of your sight, and raise this present head;
Whereby we stand opposed by such means
As you yourself have forg'd against yourself,
By unkind usage, dangerous countenance,
And violation of all faith and troth   70
Sworn to us in your younger enterprise.
KING. These things, indeed, you have articulate,
Proclaim'd at market-crosses, read in churches,

Lines 41, 'You swore
to us . . .', to 58
omitted.

To face the garment of rebellion
With some fine colour that may please the eye   75
Of fickle changelings and poor discontents,
Which gape and rub the elbow at the news
Of hurlyburly innovation;
And never yet did insurrection want
Such water-colours to impaint his cause,   80
Nor moody beggars, starving for a time
Of pellmell havoc and confusion.
PRINCE. In both your armies there is many a soul
    Shall pay full dearly for this encounter,
    If once they join in trial.   Tell your nephew   85
    The Prince of Wales doth join with all the world
    In praise of Henry Percy.   By my hopes,
    This present enterprise set off his head,
    I do not think a braver gentleman,
    More active-valiant or more valiant-young,   90
    More daring or more bold, is now alive
    To grace this latter age with noble deeds.
    For my part, I may speak it to my shame,
    I have a truant been to chivalry;
    And so I hear he doth account me too.   95
    Yet this before my father's majesty—
    I am content that he shall take the odds
    Of his great name and estimation,
    And will, to save the blood on either side,
    Try fortune with him in a single fight.   100
KING. And, Prince of Wales, so dare we venture thee,
    Albeit considerations infinite
    Do make against it.   No, good Worcester, no,
    We love our people well; even those we love
    That are misled upon your cousin's part;   105
    And will they take the offer of our grace,
    Both he and they and you, yea, every man
    Shall be my friend again, and I'll be his.
    So tell your cousin, and bring me word
    What he will do.   But if he will not yield,   110
    Rebuke and dread correction wait on us,
    And they shall do their office.   So, be gone;
    We will not now be troubled with reply.
    We offer fair; take it advisedly. [*Exeunt* WORCESTER *and* VERNON.
PRINCE. It will not be accepted, on my life: 115
    The Douglas and the Hotspur both together
    Are confident against the world in arms.
KING. Hence, therefore, every leader to his charge;
    For, on their answer, will we set on them;
    And God befriend us, as our cause is just!   120
                [*Exeunt all but the* PRINCE *and* FALSTAFF.
FAL. Hal, if thou see me down in the battle, and bestride me, so;
    'tis a point of friendship.
PRINCE. Nothing but a colossus can do thee that friendship.   Say
    thy prayers, and farewell.
FAL. I would 'twere bed-time, Hal, and all well.   125
PRINCE. Why, thou owest God a death.   [*Exit.*

FAL. 'Tis not due yet ; I would be loath to pay him before his day.
What need I be so forward with him that calls not on me ? Well,
'tis no matter ; honour pricks me on. Yea, but how if honour
prick me off when I come on ? How then ? Can honour set
to a leg ? No. Or an arm ? No. Or take away the grief of
a wound ? No. Honour hath no skill in surgery, then ? No.
What is honour ? A word. What is in that word ? Honour.
What is that honour ? Air. A trim reckoning ! Who hath it ?
He that died o' Wednesday. Doth he feel it ? No. Doth he
hear it ? No. 'Tis insensible, then ? Yea, to the dead. But
will it not live with the living ? No. Why ? Detraction will
not suffer it. Therefore I'll none of it. Honour is a mere
scutcheon. And so ends my catechism.   [*Exit.*

SCENE II. *The rebel camp.*

Enter WORCESTER *and* VERNON.

WOR. O, no, my nephew must not know, Sir Richard,
The liberal and kind offer of the King.
VER. 'Twere best he did.
WOR.   Then are we all undone.
It is not possible, it cannot be,
The King should keep his word in loving us ;   5
He will suspect us still, and find a time
To punish this offence in other faults ;
Supposition all our lives shall be stuck full of eyes,
For treason is but trusted like the fox,
Who, never so tame, so cherish'd, and lock'd up,   10
Will have a wild trick of his ancestors.
Look how we can, or sad or merrily,
Interpretation will misquote our looks,
And we shall feed like oxen at a stall,
The better cherish'd still the nearer death.   15
My nephew's trespass may be well forgot ;
It hath the excuse of youth and heat of blood,
And an adopted name of privilege—
A hare-brain'd Hotspur, govern'd by a spleen.
All his offences live upon my head   20
And on his father's : we did train him on ;
And, his corruption being ta'en from us,
We, as the spring of all, shall pay for all.
Therefore, good cousin, let not Harry know,
In any case, the offer of the King.   25
VER. Deliver what you will, I'll say 'tis so.
Here comes your cousin.

Enter HOTSPUR *and* DOUGLAS.

HOT.   My uncle is return'd :
Deliver up my Lord of Westmoreland.
Uncle, what news ?   30
WOR. The King will bid you battle presently.
DOUG. Defy him by the Lord of Westmoreland.
HOT. Lord Douglas, go you and tell him so.
DOUG. Marry, and shall, and very willingly.   [*Exit.*

SCENE 17
Exterior. The Rebel
Camp near
Shrewsbury. Dawn.

Lines 8–23 omitted.

'Here comes your
cousin' omitted.

SCENE 18
Interior. A Tent in the
Rebel Camp. Dawn.
HOTSPUR and
DOUGLAS join
WORCESTER and
VERNON.

WOR. There is no seeming mercy in the King.   35
HOT. Did you beg any ?   God forbid !
WOR. I told him gently of our grievances,
Of his oath-breaking ; which he mended thus,
By now forswearing that he is forsworn.
He calls us rebels, traitors, and will scourge   40
With haughty arms this hateful name in us.

Re-enter DOUGLAS.

DOUG. Arm, gentlemen, to arms ! for I have thrown
A brave defiance in King Henry's teeth—
And Westmoreland, that was engag'd, did bear it—
Which cannot choose but bring him quickly on.   45
WOR. The Prince of Wales stepp'd forth before the King,
And, nephew, challeng'd you to single fight.
HOT. O, would the quarrel lay upon our heads ;
And that no man might draw short breath to-day
But I and Harry Monmouth !   Tell me, tell me,   50
How show'd his tasking ?   Seem'd it in contempt ?
VER. No, by my soul, I never in my life
Did hear a challenge urg'd more modestly,
Unless a brother should a brother dare
To gentle exercise and proof of arms.   55
He gave you all the duties of a man ;
Trimm'd up your praises with a princely tongue ;
Spoke your deservings like a chronicle ;
Making you ever better than his praise,
By still dispraising praise valued with you ;   60
And, which became him like a prince indeed,
He made a blushing cital of himself,
And chid his truant youth with such a grace
As if he mast'red there a double spirit,
Of teaching and of learning instantly.   65
There did he pause ; but let me tell the world—
If he outlive the envy of this day,
England did never owe so sweet a hope,
So much misconstrued in his wantonness.
HOT. Cousin, I think thou art enamoured   70
On his follies.   Never did I hear
Of any prince so wild a liberty.
But be he as he will, yet once ere night
I will embrace him with a soldier's arm,
That he shall shrink under my courtesy.   75
Arm, arm with speed ! and, fellows, soldiers, friends,
Better consider what you have to do
Than I, that have not well the gift of tongue,
Can lift your blood up with persuasion.

Enter a Messenger.

MESS. My lord, here are letters for you.   80
HOT. I cannot read them now.
O gentlemen, the time of life is short !
To spend that shortness basely were too long,
If life did ride upon a dial's point,

Lady Percy (Michele Dotrice), Hotspur (Tim Pigott-Smith), Mortimer (Robert Morris) and Lady Mortimer (Sharon Morgan)

The Earl of Worcester (Clive Swift), Sir Richard Vernon (Terence Wilton), Hotspur (Tim Pigott-Smith) and the Earl of Douglas (John Cairney)

87

Still ending at the arrival of an hour. 85
An if we live, we live to tread on kings;
If die, brave death, when princes die with us!
Now, for our consciences, the arms are fair,
When the intent of bearing them is just.

Enter another Messenger.

MESS. My lord, prepare; the King comes on apace. 90
HOT. I thank him that he cuts me from my tale,
For I profess not talking; only this—
Let each man do his best. And here draw I
A sword, whose temper I intend to stain
With the best blood that I can meet withal 95
In the adventure of this perilous day.
Now, Esperance! Percy! and set on.
Sound all the lofty instruments of war,
And by that music let us all embrace;
For, heaven to earth, some of us never shall 100
A second time do such a courtesy.
[*They embrace. The trumpets sound. Exeunt.*

SCENE III. *A plain between the camps.*

The KING *passes across with his power. Alarum to the battle.
Then enter* DOUGLAS *and* SIR WALTER BLUNT.

BLUNT. What is thy name, that in battle thus
Thou crossest me? What honour dost thou seek
Upon my head?
DOUG. Know, then, my name is Douglas;
And I do haunt thee in the battle thus
Because some tell me that thou art a king. 5
BLUNT. They tell thee true.
DOUG. The Lord of Stafford dear to-day hath bought
Thy likeness; for instead of thee, King Harry,
This sword hath ended him. So shall it thee.
Unless thou yield thee as my prisoner. 10
BLUNT. I was not born a yielder, thou proud Scot;
And thou shalt find a king that will revenge
Lord Stafford's death. [*They fight.* DOUGLAS *kills* BLUNT.

Enter HOTSPUR.

HOT. O Douglas, hadst thou fought at Holmedon thus,
I never had triumph'd upon a Scot. 15
DOUG. All's done, all's won; here breathless lies the King.
HOT. Where?
DOUG. Here.
HOT. This, Douglas? No: I know this face full well;
A gallant knight he was, his name was Blunt; 20
Semblably furnish'd like the King himself.
DOUG. A fool go with thy soul whither it goes!
A borrowed title hast thou bought too dear;
Why didst thou tell me that thou wert a king?
HOT. The King hath many marching in his coats. 25
DOUG. Now, by my sword, I will kill all his coats;

I'll murder all his wardrobe, piece by piece,
Until I meet the King.
HOT.   Up, and away!
Our soldiers stand full fairly for the day.   [*Exeunt.*

Alarum. Enter FALSTAFF, *solus.*

FAL. Though I could scape shot-free at London, I fear the shot
here : here's no scoring but upon the pate. Soft! who are
you? Sir Walter Blunt. There's honour for you! Here's no
vanity! I am as hot as molten lead, and as heavy too. God
keep lead out of me! I need no more weight than mine own
bowels. I have led my ragamuffins where they are pepper'd ;
there's not three of my hundred and fifty left alive, and they are
for the town's end, to beg during life. But who comes here ?

Enter the PRINCE OF WALES.

PRINCE. What, stand'st thou idle here ?   Lend me thy sword.
Many a nobleman lies stark and stiff   40
Under the hoofs of vaunting enemies,
Whose deaths are yet unreveng'd.   I prithee lend me thy sword.
FAL. O Hal, I prithee give me leave to breathe awhile. Turk Gregory
never did such deeds in arms as I have done this day. I have
paid Percy, I have made him sure.   45
PRINCE. He is, indeed, and living to kill thee. I prithee lend me
thy sword.
FAL. Nay, before God, Hal, if Percy be alive, thou get'st not my
sword ; but take my pistol, if thou wilt.
PRINCE. Give it me. What, is it in the case ?   50
FAL. Ay, Hal ; 'tis hot, 'tis hot ; there's that will sack a city.
            [*The* PRINCE *draws it out, and finds it to be a bottle of sack.*
PRINCE. What, is it a time to jest and dally now ?
                        [*He throws the bottle at him. Exit.*
FAL. Well, if Percy be alive, I'll pierce him. If he do come in my
way, so ; if he do not, if I come in his willingly, let him make a
carbonado of me.   I like not such grinning honour as Sir Walter
hath.   Give me life, which if I can save, so ; if not, honour
comes unlook'd for, and there's an end.   [*Exit.*

SCENE IV. *Another part of the field.*

Alarums.   Excursions.   Enter the KING, *the* PRINCE OF WALES,
        PRINCE JOHN OF LANCASTER, *and* WESTMORELAND.

KING. I prithee,
Harry, withdraw thyself ; thou bleedest too much ;
Lord John of Lancaster, go you with him.
P. JOHN. Not I, my lord, unless I did bleed too.
PRINCE. I beseech your Majesty, make up,   5
Lest your retirement do amaze your friends.
KING. I will do so.
My Lord of Westmoreland, lead him to his tent.
WEST. Come, my lord, I'll lead you to your tent.
PRINCE. Lead me, my lord ?   I do not need your help ;   10
And God forbid a shallow scratch should drive
The Prince of Wales from such a field as this,

SCENE 20
*Exterior. Another part
of the battlefield. Day.*

Where stain'd nobility lies trodden on,
And rebels' arms triumph in massacres !
P. JOHN. We breathe too long. Come, cousin Westmoreland,   15
Our duty this way lies ; for God's sake, come.
                    [*Exeunt* PRINCE JOHN *and* WESTMORELAND.
PRINCE. By God, thou hast deceiv'd me, Lancaster !
I did not think thee lord of such a spirit ;
Before, I lov'd thee as a brother, John,
But now I do respect thee as my soul.   20
KING. I saw him hold Lord Percy at the point
With lustier maintenance than I did look for
Of such an ungrown warrior.
PRINCE.   O, this boy
Lends mettle to us all !   [*Exit.*

                    Enter DOUGLAS.

DOUG. Another king ! They grow like Hydra's heads.   25
I am the Douglas, fatal to all those
That wear those colours on them.   What art thou,
That counterfeit'st the person of a king ?
KING. The King himself, who, Douglas, grieves at heart
So many of his shadows thou hast met,   30
And not the very King.   I have two boys
Scek Percy and thyself about the field ;
But, seeing thou fall'st on me so luckily,
I will assay thee ; so, defend thyself.
DOUG. I fear thou art another counterfeit ;   35
And yet, in faith, thou bearest thee like a king ;
But mine I am sure thou art, who'er thou be,
And thus I win thee.
            [*They fight, the* KING *being in danger.*

                Re-enter the PRINCE.

PRINCE. Hold up thy head, vile Scot, or thou art like
Never to hold it up again.   The spirits   40
Of valiant Shirley, Stafford, Blunt, are in my arms ;
It is the Prince of Wales that threatens thee,
Who never promiseth but he means to pay.
                    [*They fight ;* DOUGLAS *flies.*
Cheerly, my lord : how fares your Grace ?
Sir Nicholas Gawsey hath for succour sent,   45
And so hath Clifton.   I'll to Clifton straight.
KING. Stay, and breathe awhile.
Thou hast redeem'd thy lost opinion ;
And show'd thou mak'st some tender of my life,
In this fair rescue thou hast brought to me.   50
PRINCE. O God, they did me too much injury
That ever said I heark'ned for your death !
If it were so, I might have let alone
The insulting hand of Douglas over you,
Which would have been as speedy in your end   55
As all the poisonous potions in the world,
And sav'd the treacherous labour of your son.
KING. Make up to Clifton, I'll to Sir Nicholas Gawsey.   [*Exit.*

Jon Finch as King Henry IV

Enter HOTSPUR

HOT. If I mistake not, thou art Harry Monmouth.
PRINCE. Thou speak'st as if I would deny my name.   60
HOT. My name is Harry Percy.
PRINCE.   Why, then I see
   A very valiant rebel of the name.
   I am the Prince of Wales ; and think not, Percy,
   To share with me in glory any more.
   Two stars keep not their motion in one sphere,   65
   Nor can one England brook a double reign
   Of Harry Percy and the Prince of Wales.
HOT. Nor shall it, Harry, for the hour is come
   To end the one of us ; and would to God
   Thy name in arms were now as great as mine !   70
PRINCE. I'll make it greater ere I part from thee,
   And all the budding honours on thy crest
   I'll crop to make a garland for my head.
HOT. I can no longer brook thy vanities.   [*They fight.*

Enter FALSTAFF.

FAL. Well said, Hal ! to it, Hal ! Nay, you shall find no boy's play
   here, I can tell you.   76

Re-enter DOUGLAS ; *he fights with* FALSTAFF, *who falls down as if he
   were dead ;* DOUGLAS *withdraws.* HOTSPUR *is wounded and falls.*

HOT. O, Harry, thou hast robb'd me of my youth !
   I better brook the loss of brittle life
   Than those proud titles thou hast won of me :
   They wound my thoughts worse than thy sword my flesh ;   80
   But thoughts, the slaves of life, and life, time's fool,
   And time, that takes survey of all the world,
   Must have a stop. O, I could prophesy,
   But that the earthy and cold hand of death
   Lies on my tongue. No, Percy, thou art dust   85
   And food for—   [*Dies.*
PRINCE. For worms, brave Percy. Fare thee well, great heart !
   Ill-weav'd ambition, how much art thou shrunk !
   When that this body did contain a spirit,
   A kingdom for it was too small a bound ;   90
   But now two paces of the vilest earth
   Is room enough. This earth that bears thee dead
   Bears not alive so stout a gentleman.
   If thou wert sensible of courtesy,
   I should not make so dear a show of zeal ;   95
   But let my favours hide thy mangled face,
   And, even in thy behalf, I'll thank myself
   For doing these fair rites of tenderness.
   Adieu, and take thy praise with thee to heaven !
   Thy ignominy sleep with thee in the grave,   100
   But not rememb'red in thy epitaph !
                      [*He spieth* FALSTAFF *on the ground.*
   What, old acquaintance ! Could not all this flesh
   Keep in a little life ? Poor Jack, farewell !

I could have better spar'd a better man.
O, I should have a heavy miss of thee,   105
If I were much in love with vanity!
Death hath not struck so fat a deer to-day,
Though many dearer, in this bloody fray.
Embowell'd will I see thee by and by;
Till then in blood by noble Percy lie.   [*Exit.*
FAL. [*Rising up.*] Embowell'd! If thou embowel me to-day, I'll
give you leave to powder me and eat me too to-morrow. 'Sblood,
'twas time to counterfeit, or that hot termagant Scot had paid me
scot and lot too. Counterfeit? I lie, I am no counterfeit: to die
is to be a counterfeit; for he is but the counterfeit of a man who
hath not the life of a man; but to counterfeit dying, when a man
thereby liveth, is to be no counterfeit, but the true and perfect
image of life indeed. The better part of valour is discretion; in
the which better part I have saved my life. Zounds, I am afraid
of this gunpowder Percy, though he be dead; how if he should
counterfeit too, and rise? By my faith, I am afraid he would prove
the better counterfeit. Therefore I'll make him sure; yea, and I'll
swear I kill'd him. Why may not he rise as well as I? Nothing
confutes me but eyes, and nobody sees me. Therefore, sirrah
[*stabbing him*], with a new wound in your thigh, come you along
with me.   [*He takes up* HOTSPUR *on his back.*

Re-enter the PRINCE OF WALES *and* PRINCE JOHN OF LANCASTER.

PRINCE. Come, brother John, full bravely hast thou flesh'd
    Thy maiden sword.
P. JOHN.   But, soft! whom have we here?   130
    Did you not tell me this fat man was dead?
PRINCE. I did; I saw him dead,
    Breathless and bleeding on the ground. Art thou alive?
    Or is it fantasy that plays upon our eyesight?
    I prithee speak; we will not trust our eyes   135
    Without our ears: thou art not what thou seem'st.
FAL. No, that's certain: I am not a double man; but if I be not
Jack Falstaff, then am I a Jack. There is Percy [*throwing the body
down*]; if your father will do me any honour, so; if not, let him
kill the next Percy himself. I look to be either earl or duke, I can
assure you.   141
PRINCE. Why, Percy, I kill'd myself, and saw thee dead.
FAL. Didst thou? Lord, Lord, how this world is given to lying!
I grant you I was down and out of breath, and so was he; but
we rose both at an instant, and fought a long hour by Shrewsbury
clock. If I may be believ'd, so; if not, let them that should
reward valour bear the sin upon their own heads. I'll take it
upon my death, I gave him this wound in the thigh; if the man
were alive, and would deny it, zounds, I would make him eat a
piece of my sword.
P. JOHN. This is the strangest tale that ever I heard.
PRINCE. This is the strangest fellow, brother John.
    Come, bring your luggage nobly on your back.   155
    For my part, if a lie may do thee grace,
    I'll gild it with the happiest terms I have. [*A retreat is sounded.*
    The trumpet sounds retreat; the day is ours.

Come, brother, let us to the highest of the field,
To see what friends are living, who are dead.   160
      [*Exeunt the* PRINCE *and* PRINCE JOHN OF LANCASTER.
FAL. I'll follow, as they say, for reward.   He that rewards me, God
reward him !   If I do grow great, I'll grow less ; for I'll purge,
and leave sack, and live cleanly, as a nobleman should do.   [*Exit.*

SCENE V.   *Another part of the field.*

SCENE 21
*Exterior. Another part
of the battlefield. Day.*

The Trumpets sound.   Enter the KING, *the* PRINCE OF WALES, PRINCE
JOHN OF LANCASTER, WESTMORELAND, *with* WORCESTER *and* VERNON
prisoners.

KING. Thus ever did rebellion find rebuke.
    Ill-spirited Worcester ! did not we send grace,
    Pardon and terms of love to all of you ?
    And wouldst thou turn our offers contrary ?
    Misuse the tenour of thy kinsman's trust ?   5
    Three knights upon our party slain to-day,
    A noble earl, and many a creature else,
    Had been alive this hour,
    If like a Christian thou hadst truly borne
    Betwixt our armies true intelligence.   10
WOR. What I have done my safety urg'd me to ;
    And I embrace this fortune patiently,
    Since not to be avoided it falls on me.
KING. Bear Worcester to the death, and Vernon too ;
    Other offenders we will pause upon.   15
        [*Exeunt* WORCESTER *and* VERNON *guarded.*
    How goes the field ?
PRINCE. The noble Scot, Lord Douglas, when he saw
    The fortune of the day quite turn'd from him,
    The noble Percy slain, and all his men
    Upon the foot of fear, fled with the rest ;   20
    And falling from a hill, he was so bruis'd
    That the pursuers took him.   At my tent
    The Douglas is ; and I beseech your Grace
    I may dispose of him.
KING.   With all my heart.
PRINCE. Then, brother John of Lancaster, to you   25
    This honourable bounty shall belong :
    Go to the Douglas, and deliver him
    Up to his pleasure, ransomless and free ;
    His valours shown upon our crests to-day
    Have taught us how to cherish such high deeds   30
    Even in the bosom of our adversaries.
P. JOHN. I thank your Grace for this high courtesy,
    Which I shall give away immediately.
KING. Then this remains—that we divide our power.
    You, son John, and my cousin Westmoreland,   35
    Towards York shall bend you with your dearest speed
    To meet Northumberland and the prelate Scroop,
    Who, as we hear, are busily in arms.
    Myself, and you, son Harry, will towards Wales

To fight with Glendower and the Earl of March.   40
Rebellion in this land shall lose his sway,
Meeting the check of such another day ;
And since this business so fair is done,
Let us not leave till all our own be won.   *[Exeunt.*

GLOSSARY

Scott Shane

Difficult phrases are listed under the most important or most difficult word in them. If no such word stands out, they are listed under the first word.

Words appear in the form they take in the text. If they occur in several forms, they are listed under the root form (singular for nouns, infinitive for verbs).

Line references are given only when the same word is used with different meanings, and when there are puns.

Line numbers for prose passages are counted from the last numbered line before the line referred to (since the numbers given do not always correspond to those in this edition).

'A, he
ACCENTS, words
ACCIDENTS, 'rare accidents', infrequent and unexpected events
ACTION, (i) encounter (II iv 18); (ii) battle (i.e. the robbery and its aftermath) (III iii 1)
ADMIRAL, flagship
ADOPTED NAME OF PRIVILEGE, nickname which licenses his rashness
ADVANTAGE, 'at more advantage', at a more convenient time; 'with advantage', with interest; 'Advantage feeds him fat', i.e. the rebels' advantage grows
ADVENTURE, hazard (V ii 96)
ADVERTISEMENT, (i) news (III ii 172); (ii) advice (IV i 36)
ADVISEDLY, with careful consideration
AFFECTIONS, inclinations
AFOOT, on foot
AFORE, before
AFRONT, abreast
AGAINST HIS NAME, to the detriment of his reputation
AGUES, fevers
AIM'D, planned
ALARUM, trumpet-call signalling the advance into battle
ALL IS ONE FOR THAT, that makes no difference
ALL-HALLOWN SUMMER, good weather as late as All Saints' Day (1 November), i.e. youthful ways retained in old age

AMAIMON, a devil to whom Glendower has supposedly given a beating on the soles of the feet ('the bastinado')
AMAZE, bewilder
AMENDMENT, reformation
AN, if; 'An if', even if, if indeed
ANCIENT, (i) ensign (IV ii 21); (ii) flag (IV ii 28)
ANGEL, 'makes an angel', will bring your debt up to one angel or ten shillings (but Falstaff takes the phrase to mean 'coins an angel')
ANOINTED, i.e. with consecrated oil at his coronation
ANON, soon, in a minute; 'ever and anon', now and again
ANSWER THE COINAGE, guarantee that the 'angels' are not counterfeit
ANTIC, clown
APACE, rapidly
APPLE-JOHN, kind of apple, eaten after the skin has wrinkled
APPOINTMENT, piece of dress or equipment
APPROVE, test
APPROVED, proved in battle, tested
ARBITREMENT, impartial scrutiny
ARGUMENT, subject matter (for conversation, II ii 90; for the play, II iv 272)
ARRANT, thoroughgoing, absolute
ARRAS, wall-hanging, tapestry
ART, magic
ARTICULATE, described in detail
ASPECT, appearance

ASSAY, try
ATHWART, thwarting our purposes
ATTEMPTS, exploits
ATTRIBUTION, praise
AUDIENCE, 'Give me audience', listen to me
AUDITOR, revenue officer
AWAY, 'must away all night', must march all night long
AXLE-TREE, axle of a cart

BACK, mount
BACONS, fat men
BAFFLE, disgrace publicly (a perjured knight was 'baffled' or hung upside down in public)
BALD, trivial
BALK'D, (i) lying in ridges (like the 'balks' that separate furrows in a field); (ii) thwarted (pun, I i 69)
BALLADS, i.e. scurrilous ballads, as were often composed about notorious criminals
BANDS, bonds, pledges
BANNS, 'ask'd twice on the banns', i.e. their public announcement of intention to marry had been made two out of the usual three times
BARBARY, i.e. where Francis might run to (this and the preceding seem to be near-nonsense mainly aimed at mystifying Francis)
BARENESS, (i) lack of clothes; (ii) leanness (pun, IV ii 69)
BASE-STRING, lowest note
BASILISKS, very large cannons
BASTARD, sweet Spanish wine
BATE, (i) lose weight (III iii 2); (ii) flutter their wings (IV i 99)
BATTLE, army (IV i 129)
BAVIN, brushwood (which flares up and burns out quickly)
BEARD, challenge
BEARS, 'bears hard', resents; 'bears his mind', contain his message
BEAT CUT'S SADDLE, beat the work-horse's saddle to soften it
BEAVER, helmet
BECOME NOT A CART, do not look as fine in the cart to the gallows
BEGUILE, cheat
BEHALF, 'in an unjust behalf', for an unjust cause
BEHOLDING, indebted
BELDAM, grandmother
BELIE, misrepresent
BESIDES, out of (III i 179)
BESLUBBER, smear

BESTRIDE ME, i.e. stand over me and protect me
BEND YOU, direct your course
BESPOKE, arranged for
BETIMES, early
BETTER WORTH, worth more
BETWIXT, between
BEWARE, take note of
BIDE THE TOUCH, be put to the test (as metal is tested by a touchstone)
BIG, 'look big Upon', threaten
BIRD, nestling, young bird
BLOOD, (i) spirit (III i 181, IV iii 76, V ii 79); (ii) offspring (III ii 6)
BLOT, moral stain
BLOWN, (i) swollen; (ii) breathless (pun, IV ii 47)
BLUE-CAPS, Scots
BOLTERS, flour-sifters
BOLTING-HUTCH, sifting-bin (in which 'beastliness' collects like the impurities in flour)
BOMBARD, leather wine jug
BOMBAST, (i) cotton or wool stuffing; (ii) high-flown language (pun, II iv 318)
BONDS, documents promising the payment of debts
BOOK, (i) Bible (II iv 46); (ii) i.e. the agreement (III i 223, 265)
BOOTLESS, profitless
BOOTS, (i) boots; (ii) booty (pun, II i 79)
BOSOM, 'into the bosom creep', work your way into the confidences
BOTS, stomach worms
BOTTOM, 'so rich a bottom', so valuable a valley; 'very bottom', full extent
BOUNTY, generosity
BRACH, bitch (apparently an Irish wolfhound)
BRAVE, fine
BRAWLING, shouting
BRAWN, fat pig
BREAK, 'break my wind', be altogether out of breath; 'Break with', inform
BREATHE, (i) utter (I i 3); (ii) pause for breath (I iii 102, II iv 14, V iii 43, V iv 15, 47)
BREWER'S HORSE, i.e. scrawny and worn out (old horses were used by brewers to turn the malt grindstone)
BRIEF, letter
BRING IN, a command to a waiter in a tavern to bring food and drink
BRISK, smartly dressed
BROACHED MISCHIEF, evil let loose
BROIL, battle, strife

BROOK, tolerate
BUCKLER, small shield
BUCKRAM, coarse linen stiffened with gum
BUFF JERKIN, close-fitting leather jacket
BUFFETING, 'civil buffeting hold', civil war last
BURGOMASTERS, town councillors, aldermen
BUSKY, bushy
BUTTER, i.e. fat (IV ii 58)
BY-DRINKINGS, drinks between meals
BY-ROOM, adjoining room

CADDIS-GARTER, inexpensive worsted garter
CALIVER, light musket
CAMBYSES, 'King Cambyses' vein', the ranting manner of the hero of Thomas Preston's primitive tragedy *Cambyses* (1569)
CAMOMILE, aromatic herb
CANDY DEAL, sugary quantity
CANKER (n.), (i) dog-rose (an inferior wild rose); (ii) worm, parasite (IV ii 26); (iii) ulcer, sore (pun on (i), (ii), and (iii), I iii 176)
CANK'RED, corrupt
CANSTICK, 'brazen canstick turn'd', brass candlestick being fashioned on a lathe
CANTLE, piece
CAP AND KNEE, cap removed and on bended knee
CAPITULATE, league together
CARBONADO, piece of meat sliced open for broiling
CARDED HIS STATE, mixed his dignity with baseness
CARRIAGE, bearing
CARRIER, coach-driver
CARRIES YOU AWAY, (i) requires that you leave home; (ii) transports you, excites you (pun, II iii 72)
CASE YE, put on your masks
CASES OF BUCKRAM, outer suits of rough cloth
CAST, throw of the dice
CASTLE, 'old lad of the castle', (i) old scoundrel; (ii) frequenter of the Castle, a notorious London brothel (with further pun on Falstaff's original name, 'Oldcastle'); 'as in a castle, cocksure', with complete security and confidence
CATECHISM, set of questions and answers used for instruction in Christian faith
CATES, delicacies
CAVIL, raise petty objections

CESS, 'out of all cess', beyond reckoning
CHAMBERLAIN, servant in charge of rooms at an inn
CHAMBER-LYE, urine
CHANCE OF WAR, misfortune of military defeat
CHANDLER'S, candlemaker's
CHANGELINGS, inconstant people
CHARGE, (i) expense (I iii 79, III i 112, 115); (ii) luggage, valuables (II i 45, 56); (iii) command of troops (III ii 161, III iii 200, IV ii 21, V i 118); (iv) assignment (IV iii 41); 'limits of the charge', assignments of duties and expenses; 'charge of foot', command of a company of foot-soldiers
CHARING CROSS, a village (at the time of the play) on the far side of London from Rochester
CHARLES' WAIN, the Great Bear or Big Dipper
CHEERLY, have good cheer
CHEESE AND GARLIC, i.e. bad smells
CHEWET, (i) jackdaw, chatterer; (ii) meat pie (pun, V i 29)
CHID, scolded
CHIMNEY, fireplace (II i 18)
CHOLER, anger
CHOOSE, 'I cannot choose', I cannot help it
CHOPS, i.e. fat-cheeks
CHRISTEN, Christian; 'ne'er a king christen', i.e. not even a Christian king (who would have the most of everything)
CHRONICLE, 'like a chronicle', with accuracy and detail
CHUFFS, misers
CHURLISH, rude, brutal
CITAL, 'blushing cital of', ashamed account of
CIVIL, (i) between citizens of one country (I i 13, II iv 351); (ii) gentle, orderly (IV iii 43)
CLAP TO, shut
CLEANLY, skilful (II iv 439)
CLIPP'D IN WITH, enclosed by
CLOAK-BAG, suitcase
CLOSE (adv.), 'stand close', hide; 'keep close', keep to yourself; (n.), hand-to-hand combat
CLOSER, more tight-mouthed
CLOUDY, sullen (but they are also 'clouds' obscuring the 'sun-like' king)
COCK, 'the first cock', midnight
COFFERS, money-chests
COLOUR (n.), (i) colour; (ii) pretext (pun, V i 75); 'colour like to', persuasive pretence of; (v.), (i) disguise; (ii) colour with blood (pun, I iii 109)

COLT, trick (with pun on 'colted', possessed of a horse, II ii 35)

COME AWAY, come here

COMFIT-MAKER'S, confectioner's

COMMODITY, 'commodity of good names', supply of good reputations; 'commodity of warm slaves', collection of comfortable cowards

COMMON-HACKNEY'D, cheapened, vulgarised

COMMUNITY, familiarity

COMPANY, 'will along with company', wish to travel together (for safety)

COMPARATIVE (adj.), abusive, fond of insulting comparisons; (n.), 'beardless vain comparative', young and conceited wit

COMPASS, (i) moderation (III iii 19–20); (ii) girth, size (III iii 22)

COMPOUND, combination (of sun and butter)

CONCEALMENTS, magical arts

CONDITION, mild natural disposition (v. 'myself', my necessary sternness and power as king)

CONFOUND, spend

CONFUTES, 'Nothing confutes me but eyes', nothing can disprove my story but an eyewitness

CONJUNCTION, united forces

CONTAGIOUS, disease-carrying (as clouds were believed to be)

CONTENT, agreed

CONTINENT, 'Gelding the opposed continent', cutting off from the opposite bank

CONTRACTED, engaged to marry

CONTRARIOUS, adverse, in the wrong direction

CONVERSE, associate

CONVEY, accompany out of the room

CORINTHIAN, good fellow, drinking companion

CORPSE, bodies

CORPULENT, full-bodied

CORRIVAL, (i) rival (I iii 207); (ii) ally of equal worth (IV iv 31)

CORSE, corpse

COUCHING, crouching

COUNTENANCE, 'under whose countenance', (i) under whose face, i.e. the moon; (ii) under whose protection (pun, I ii 27); 'want countenance', lack patronage; 'holds his countenance', keeps a straight face; 'gave his countenance', (i) presented his face; (ii) permitted himself (pun, III ii 65); 'dangerous countenance', menacing looks

COUNTERPOISE, 'for the counterpoise of', to outweigh (in military strength)

COUSIN, COZ, kinsman (a title of respect not always indicating a blood relationship)

COZENERS, deceivers (with pun on 'cousin', I iii 255)

COZENING, cheating

CRANKING, 'comes me cranking in', winds into my portion

CREDIT SAKE, reputation's sake

CRESSETS, iron fire-baskets mounted on poles as torches

CREST, (i) 'bristle up the crest', show the proud hostility (I i 99); (ii) coat of arms on a helmet (V iv 72); (iii) helmet (V v 29)

CRISP HEAD, rippled stream (resembling the 'crisp' curls of a man's head)

CROP-EAR, horse with the ears trimmed short

CROSSEST, oppose

CROSSINGS, contradictions

CROWNS, gold coins (I ii 126); 'crack'd crowns', (i) broken heads; (ii) usurped kingships; (iii) damaged gold coins (pun, II iii 90)

CRY YOU MERCY, beg your pardon

CULVERIN, small cannons

CUNNING, clever

CURRENT (adj.), 'Come current for', be accepted as; 'holds current', is still true; 'go so general current', be so widely honoured

CURRENTS (n.), actions

CURS'D, bed-tempered

CUSHES, thigh-armour

CUT ME, cut

DAFF'D THE WORLD ASIDE, tossed all serious business aside

DANK . . . AS A DOG, very soggy

DARE, daring (IV i 78)

DATE IS OUT, term has expired

DAUB, paint, defile

DEAL, quantity

DEALT, dealt blows, fought

DEAR, (i) important (I i 33, IV i 34); (ii) valuable (IV iv 31); (iii) heartfelt (V iv 95)

DEARER, nobler, more valuable militarily

DEAREST, (i) most loved; (ii) direst, bitterest (pun, III ii 123)

DEATH'S HEAD, skull (frequently engraved on jewellery)

DEFEND, 'God defend', God forbid

DEFY, (i) renounce (I iii 228); (ii) despise (IV i 6)

DELIVER, (i) report, tell (I iii 26, V ii 26); (ii)

'deliver up', hand over (I iii 260, V ii 28, V v 27)

DENIER, one-tenth of a penny

DEPUTATION, 'by deputation', by a substitute; 'In deputation', as his deputies

DEPUTY'S WIFE OF THE WARD, i.e. the height of respectability

DETERMINATION, side in the conflict

DETRACTION, slander

DEVICE, stratagem, trick

DEVIL RIDES UPON A FIDDLE-STICK, what's all the fuss about? (proverbial)

DIALS, sundials

DIAL'S POINT, 'If life . . . hour', even if life lasted only one hour

DIANA'S FORESTERS, huntsmen (i.e. thieves) serving the goddess of the moon, the hunt, and chastity

DISCARDED, dismissed from service

DISCOMFITED, defeated

DISDAIN'D, disdainful

DISLIKE, discord (V i 26)

DISPRAISING PRAISE VALUED WITH YOU, claiming that his praises fell far short of your deserving

DISTEMP'RATURE, physical disorder, unhealthy state

DITTY, lyric poem

DIVERS, various

DIVES, the rich man in Luke xvi 19–31 who burns in hell

DIVIDE MYSELF AND GO TO BUFFETTS, split myself in two and have one half beat the other

DIVISION, melody (III i 210)

DOFF, remove

DOOM, judgement

DOUBLE MAN, (i) ghost; (ii) deceitful man; (iii) two men (with Hotspur's body) (pun, V iv 137)

DOUBLET, close-fitting jacket

DOUBT, fear

DOWLAS, coarse linen

DRAFF, pig-swill

DRAW, gather (IV i 33, 126)

DRAWER, tapster, waiter in a tavern

DRAWN FOX, fox drawn from its den and thus using all its cunning to save itself

DRENCH, dose of medicine

DRIVE AWAY, pass pleasantly

DRONE, continuous bass note

DROPSIES, disease-causing bodily fluids

DROWZ'D, dozed

DURANCE, 'of durance', (i) durable, long-lasting; (ii) suggesting imprisonment (because 'buff jerkins' were worn by the sheriff's officers) (pun, I ii 41)

DUTIES OF, respect due to

DYEING SCARLET, (i) getting a drinker's red complexion; (ii) contributing the urine which was used in the dye process (pun, II iv 13)

EASTCHEAP, street and district in London

EBREW JEW, out-and-out Jew

ECCE SIGNUM, behold the evidence

ELL, 45 inches

EMBOSS'D RASCAL, (i) swollen scoundrel; (ii) rascal, or lean deer, which is foaming at the mouth (pun, III iii 156)

EMBOWELL'D, disembowelled (for embalming)

ENFEOFF'D, surrendered

ENFORC'D, forced

ENGAGE, (i) pledge (I i 21, II iv 496); (ii) 'engag'd', held as hostage (IV iii 95, V ii 44)

ENGROSS UP, buy up, amass

ENLARGED, released

ENLARGEMENT, release

ENTERTAIN, occupy

ENTRANCE, surface

ENVY, malice (I iii 27, V ii 67)

EQUITY, 'no equity stirring', no correct judgement in the world

ERE, before

ESPERANCE, hope (the motto and battle-cry of the Percy family)

ESSENTIALLY MADE, of a truly royal nature (Falstaff apparently begs Hal not to turn him over to the Sheriff: he is 'true' gold, not counterfeit, as Hal is true royalty, though he does not seem so)

ESTIMATION, 'in estimation', as a guess; 'estimation and command', reputation and skill; 'great name and estimation', great reputation

EVEN, carefully, correctly (I iii 285)

EXCHEQUER, royal treasury

EXCURSIONS, sorties, charges

EXECUTE, be performed

EXHALATIONS, fiery meteors, i.e. pimples on Bardolph's face

EXHAL'D, (i) drawn out of earthly vapours by the sun; (ii) dragged off its rightful orbit (pun, V i 19)

EXPECTATION, promise

EXPEDIENCE, 'dear expedience', important expedition

EXPEDITION, enterprise

EXTEMPORE, impromptu, without rehearsal; 'blushed extempore', i.e. because of your drinker's complexion

EXTENUATION, mitigation, forgiveness

EXTREMITIES, great dangers

FACE (n.), assumed guise of the people's advocate (IV iii 82); (v.), adorn, trim ornamentally (V i 74)

FACTION, 'fearful faction', timid supporters

FACTOR, agent

FAITH, reliability (II i 30)

FALL, 'fall off', fail in duty; 'fall'n away', shrunken, grown thin

FANTASY, hallucination

FAT, stuffy (II iv 1)

FATHOM-LINE, line used for sounding the depth of the ocean

FAT-WITTED, thick-witted

FAVOURS, (i) features (III ii 136); (ii) personal emblems (probably either ostrich plumes or a band of silk in his colours) (V iv 96)

FEAR, fear for (IV i 24, IV ii 56)

FEELING DISPUTATION, conversation full of feeling

FIGURES, figures of speech, imaginings

FILL THE MOUTH OF DEEP DEFIANCE UP, feed and increase (or enlarge the noise made by) rebellion

FINSBURY, park near London, frequented by the middle class whose genteel manners Hotspur ridicules

FIRE, i.e. fiery complexion (II iv 307)

FLAT, certain

FLESH'D THY MAIDEN SWORD, initiated your previously unused sword in the enemies' flesh

FLOCKS IN THE POINT, tufts of wool padding in the saddle-bow

FLOW'RETS, small flowers

FOIL, contrasting setting of a gem

FOOD FOR POWDER, i.e. bodies to be shot at

FOOL, 'A fool', i.e. the name of fool; 'time's fool', time's plaything

FOOT, 'foot landrakers', roaming vagabonds; 'charge of foot', command of a company of foot-soldiers; 'Upon the foot of fear', retreating in terror

FORCE, 'of force', of necessity

FORETHINK, foretell mentally

FORM, substance, point

FORSOOTH, indeed

FORSWEAR, (i) swear off, give up (I ii 178, II ii 13); (ii) swear falsely (V ii 39)

FORWARD, (i) 'so forward', taken so far (II ii 46); (ii) eager (V i 128)

FOUND ME, found me out

FOUR BY THE DAY, four o'clock in the morning

FRAMED TO THE HARP, wrote a harp accompaniment for

FRANKLIN, wealthy landowner

FRAY, battle

FRETFUL, (i) anxious; (ii) worn (or 'fretted') away (pun, III iii 11)

FRETS LIKE GUMMED VELVET, (i) wears away like velvet on which the pile has been stiffened with gum; (ii) fumes with anger (pun, II ii 2)

FRONT (v.), confront

FRONT OF HEAVEN, sky

FRONTIER, rampart; 'moody frontier of a servant brow', resentful challenge by a subject

FUBB'D, cheated, thwarted

FURNITURE, equipment

GADSHILL, place near Rochester in Kent, notorious for robberies (from which the character Gadshill takes his name)

GAGE, pledge

GALL AND PINCH, irritate and harass

GAMMON, side

GAPE, stare open-mouthed

GARTERS, 'Hang thyself in thine own heir-apparent garters', Falstaff's adaptation of a proverbial curse to Hal, who was a Knight of the Garter

GENTLEMEN OF COMPANIES, gentlemen volunteers without formal rank

GIB CAT, tom cat

GIBBETS, gallows

GILD IT WITH THE HAPPIEST TERMS, back it up with the most favourable language

GIVEN OVER, i.e. to wickedness

GIVING DIRECTION, (i) supervising the other servants' 'labouring'; (ii) planning the robbers' 'labouring' (pun, II i 49)

GLUTTON'S, i.e. Dives'

GO, 'go by', (i) work and travel by; (ii) tell time by (pun, I ii 13); 'Go to', expression of disagreement or impatience

GOD'S, 'God's body', by God's body; 'God's me', God save me; 'God's light', by God's light (all oaths)

GOLDEN, joyous (IV iii 73)

GOOD CHEAP, cheaply

GORBELLIED, pot-bellied

GOVERNMENT, (i) self-control (III i 184); (ii) command (IV i 19)

GRACE, (i) Majesty; (ii) refined manners; (iii) divine grace, salvation; (iv) grace said before a meal (pun on the first four meanings, I ii 16); (v) honour (II i 68, V iv 156); (vi) pardon (V i 106, V v 2)

GRANDAM, grandmother

GRAND-JURORS, i.e. well-to-do

GRIEF, (i) pain (I iii 51, V i 131); (ii) grievance (IV iii 42, 48)

GRIFFIN, legendary beast, half-lion and half-eagle

GRIPE THE GENERAL SWAY, seize power over the whole realm

GROSS, obvious (II iv 218)

GULL, nestling, young bird (cuckoos lay their eggs in other birds' nests, and the young cuckoos are said to destroy the other nestlings)

GYVES, shackles worn by prisoners

HABITS, clothing

HAIR, nature (IV i 61)

HALF-FAC'D FELLOWSHIP, miserable sharing of honour

HALF-MOON, name of a room in the tavern

HALF-SWORD, 'at half-sword', at close quarters

HALTER, hangman's noose (at II iv 316, taking 'choler', in the preceding line, as 'collar')

HAPPY MAN BE HIS DOLE, may each man receive happiness (proverbial)

HARD, strong (I ii 175); 'bears hard', resents; 'hard by', nearby

HARDIMENT, 'changing hardiment', exchanging valiant blows

HARE, proverbially a melancholy animal

HARE-BRAIN'D, impulsive

HARK (YOU, YE), listen

HARLOTRY, (i) rascally, good-for-nothing (II iv 384); (ii) silly wench (not suggesting sexual laxity) (III i 198)

HARNESS, armed men

HARVEST-HOME, harvest time

HAZARD, (i) chance; (ii) game using dice (pun, IV i 48); 'make a hazard of my head', (i) risk being executed; (ii) risk losing my rationality (pun, I iii 128)

HEAD, army; 'raising of a head', (i) raising an army; (ii) 'razing', i.e. removing, King Henry's head (pun, I iii 284); 'made head', led his army; 'make a head', raise an army;

'head of safety', army for our own protection

HEADY, fierce

HEARK'NED FOR, desired

HEART, 'out of heart', (i) despressed; (ii) in poor condition (pun, III iii 5)

HEAT OF BLOOD, impetuous temperament

HEAVEN TO EARTH, i.e. the odds are very great

HEAVENLY-HARNESS'D TEAM, the horses pulling the chariot of Phoebus, the sun

HEAVY, (i) distressing and weighty (I i 37, II iii 60); (ii) burdensome (IV iii 80)

HEDGE, i.e. where linen was spread out to dry

HELM, helmet

HERALD'S COAT, sleeveless coat

HERCULES, hero of extraordinary strength and valour in Greek mythology

HEST, effort

HIE, hurry

HIGHLY PENN'D, elegantly written

HIND, peasant

HIT IT, described him exactly

HITHERTO, to this spot

HOB-NAILS, short nails used in the soles of shoes or boots

HOGSHEADS, casks of liquor

HOLD, 'it holds well', it's an appropriate comparison; 'hold in', (i) keep secrets; (ii) stick together; (iii) stick close to the quarry (pun, II in 73); 'hold out water in foul way', keep your feet dry in a muddy road (i.e. protect you when you are in trouble); 'holds his countenance', keeps a straight face; 'hold me pace', keep up with me; 'hold their level', put themselves on an equal level; 'hold a wing', follow a path

HOLIDAY, elegant, not everyday

HOLLA, shout

HOLLAND, fine linen

HOLMEDON, Humbleton in Northumberland

HOLP, helped

HOLY-ROOD DAY, Holy-Cross Day, 14 September

HOME, 'pay us home', pay us in full, i.e. kill us

'HOMO' IS A COMMON NAME TO ALL MEN, i.e. honest men and thieves are all human beings ('homo' is Latin for 'man')

HOPES, 'falsify men's hopes', prove men's expectations to be false; 'By my hopes', by my hope of salvation

HORSE, (i) horses (II ii 2, IV iii 19); (ii) ass, knave (II iv 185)

HOSE, tight-fitting trousers

HOT IN QUESTION, being fervently discussed

HOUSE, (i) family (I iii 10, II iii 2, 4, 5, V i 31); (ii) inn (II i 8, 13, II iv 248, 490, 500, III iii 53, 57, 62, 97)

HOUSEHOLDERS, YEOMEN'S SONS, i.e. those well-off enough to pay to avoid military service

HUE AND CRY, general pursuit

HUMOROUS, capricious (in learning Welsh, or in playing music, or both)

HUMOUR, (i) inclinication (I ii 67, 189); (ii) whim (II iv 89–90, III i 235); 'come 'cross his humour', object to his interest in magic

HURLYBURLY INNOVATION, tumultuous rebellion

HYBLA, ancient town in Sicily, famous for its honey

HYDRA, mythological monster which grew two new heads for each one cut off

IDLENESS, foolishness, frivolity

IGNIS FATUIS, phosphorescent light seen hovering over swampy ground at night

IGNOMINY, dishonour (as a rebel)

ILL-SPIRITED, evil-minded

ILL-WEAV'D, (i) shaped by and from evil; (ii) badly woven (and therefore liable to shrink) (pun, V iv 88)

IMAGES, gilded representations of saints or warriors

IMMASK, hide

IMPAWN'D SOME SURETY, pledged some guarantee (by exchange of hostages)

IMPEACH, discredit, accuse him for

IMPORT, 'thus did it import', this was what it said; 'how much they do import', how important they are

IMPRESSED AND ENGAGED, conscripted and pledged (by the oath made in *Richard II*, V vi 49)

INCOMPREHENSIBLE, unlimited, infinite

INCURSIONS, 'hot incursions', fierce military campaigns

INDENT WITH FEARS, bargain with (i) those whose treason frightens us, and (ii) cowards

INDENTURE, (i) contract between master and apprentice (II iv 45); (ii) 'indentures tripartite', three-way agreements (III i 80, 141, 261)

INDIRECT, (i) corrupt; (ii) not inherited (pun, IV iii 105)

INDIRECTLY, without attention

INDUCTION, beginning

INDUSTRY IS, entire activity is running

INFIDEL, faithless person

INGRATE, ungrateful

INJURIES, (i) articles the loss of which would injure you (III iii 159); (ii) evils (V i 50)

INORDINATE, unrestrained

INSENSIBLE, imperceptible to the senses

INSTANT, immediate; 'at an instant', at once

INSTANTLY, simultaneously

INSULTING, contemptuously exultant

INTELLIGENCE, (i) spies (IV iii 98); (ii) information (V v 10)

INTEMPERATURE, (i) wild behaviour; (ii) illness (pun, III ii 156)

INTENDED, ready to set forth

INTERCHANGEABLY, i.e. each copy by all three parties

INTEREST, 'worthy interest to the state', claim to the monarchy by virtue of worth

INTESTINE, internal

IRON, merciless, cruel

IRREGULAR AND WILD, fighting lawlessly, like a guerrilla

ISSUE, outcome, result

INTERATION, quotation of Scripture

JACK, knave, rude fellow (with puns on Falstaff's name)

JADE, nag, poor horse

JERKIN, close-fitting jacket, which might have 'crystal buttons' (this and what follows refer to the middle-class dress and manners of the tavernkeeper) (II iv 66)

JOHN OF GAUNT, Prince Hal's grandfather, noted for valour (with pun on Hal's 'gaunt' physique)

JOIN'D-STOOL, wooden stool made by a joiner, or cabinetmaker

JORDAN, chamber-pot

JOURNEY-BATED, exhausted by travel

JOYED, was glad

JUMPS WITH MY HUMOUR, suits my inclination

JURE YE, comic coinage based on 'juror', without a specific meaning

JUSTLING, turbulent

KEEP, (i) dwell (I iii 244); (ii) make (II ii 6); (iii) stay in (IV i 21)

KENDAL GREEN, coarse green cloth

KIND, way (I iii 121)

KNIGHT OF THE BURNING LAMP, i.e. knight of the red and pimpled face

KNOT-PATED, short-haired
KNOTTY-PATED, thick-headed

LADDER, i.e. the ladder leading to the gallows
LADY, ladylike, effeminate
LAG-END, latter part
LANCASTER, i.e. King Henry (III i 8)
LANES, rows
LARDS, greases, fattens (sweat was believed to be melted fat)
LATE, recently
LATH, 'dagger of lath', wooden sword (with which the character called the Vice attacked the devil in morality plays)
LATTER SPRING, i.e. youthful ways retained in old age
LAY, 'Lay by', the cry of robbers to their victims; 'thou layest the plot how', you plan how it is done (both the servants' work and the robbers' work); 'lay open', reveal; 'here I lay', here I stood; 'Lay out', pay for it yourself
LAZARUS, the beggar in the parable of Dives, Luke xvi 19–31
LEADING, qualities of leadership
LEAGUE, about three miles
LEAK, urinate
LEAPING-HOUSES, brothels
LEASH OF DRAWERS, trio of tapsters
LEAVE (n.), permission; (v.), stop (II iv 27, V v 44)
LEG, bow (II iv 377)
LET, 'let him', let him go; 'let'st slip', let the hounds loose (a rebuke to Hotspur's reckless haste); 'let drive at', came for
LEWD, worthless
LEWDLY GIVEN, inclined to wickedness
LIBERTY, reckless freedom of conduct
LICENSE, grant permission for
LIEF, gladly
LIEGE, lord
LIEGEMAN, subject, servant
LIFT YOUR BLOOD UP, incite you to passionate spirit
LIGHT, (i) dismount (I i 63); (ii) 'light on', come upon (II ii 59); (iii) dawn (III ii 138)
LIKE (adj.), (i) likely (I ii 168, II iv 351, 354, III ii 124, IV iv 7, V iv 39); (ii) similar (III ii 100); (v.), please (II iv 407)
LIKELIHOOD, promise (III ii 45); 'shape of likelihood', probability, the most likely course of events
LIKENESS, 'dear today hath bought Thy likeness', paid a high price for resembling you

LIKING, 'in some liking', (i) in the mood; (ii) fairly plump, in good condition (pun, III iii 5)
LIME, added to poor wine to make it sparkle
LIMIT, region (III i 73); 'limits of the charge', assignments of duties and costs; 'out of limit and true rule', rejecting bonds of allegiance and loyal conduct
LINE (n.), (i) level (with pun on hangman's 'cords', I iii 168); (ii) category (III ii 85); (v.), strengthen
LINKS, small torches
LION, believed traditionally never to harm a king or prince
LIQUOR'D, (i) greased (to make waterproof); (ii) bribed; (iii) made drunk (pun, II i 82)
LIST (n.), 'very list', utmost limit; (v.), listen
LIVE UPON, are blamed upon
LIVERS, 'Hot livers and cold purses', i.e. two results of excessive drinking
LOACH, 'like a loach', as a loach (a kind of fish) breeds loaches, i.e. in great quantity
LOADEN, burdened
LOGGERHEADS, blockheads
LONG-GROWN, long-standing, habitual
LONG-STAFF SIXPENNY STRIKERS, staff-carrying petty thieves
LOOK FOR, LOOK TO, expect
LOOP, loophole
LUCIFER, 'made Lucifer cuckold', caused the horns to grow on Lucifer's head
LUGG'D, chained and baited by dogs
LYING OFF, starting

MADCAP, wild, wild person
MAID MARIAN, disreputable woman in May-Day morris dances (who is the height of respectability, says Falstaff, compared to the Hostess)
MAID OF SMOKY WAR, Bellona, goddess of war
MAIDENHEAD, (i) virginity (which will be 'cheap' because all the marriageable men will have gone to war) (II iv 352); (ii) early stages (IV i 59)
MAILED, armoured
MAIM, crippling injury
MAIN, (i) stake in gambling; (ii) army (pun, IV i 47)
MAINLY, violently
MAINTENANCE, 'lustier maintenance', more vigorous resistance
MAJOR, (i) major logical premise; (ii) mayor (pronounced identically), i.e. sheriff (pun, II iv 478)

MAJORITY, 'chief majority and military title capital', pre-eminence and the name of supreme military commander

MAKE, 'make one', take part (in the robbery); 'make us all', make all our fortunes; 'make strong', gather our strength; 'make against it', argue against it; 'make up', advance

MALEVOLENT . . . IN ALL ASPECTS, evilly disposed in every way (like a star that is astrologically unfavourable)

MAMMETS, dolls

MANAGE, 'terms of manage', horseman's commands

MANNER, sort (II iv 282, 407); 'taken with the manner', caught red-handed (legal expression)

MANNINGTREE, site in Essex of an annual fair which included roasting of large oxen

MARCH OF TWELVE-SCORE, march of twelve score paces

MARK (n.), (i) coin worth thirteen shillings fourpence (two-thirds of a pound) (II i 54, II iv 502, III iii 40, 80); (ii) renown (III ii 45); 'God save the mark', here, an expression of impatient scorn; (v.), (i) pay attention to; (ii) 'mark'd For', destined to be (III ii 9–10)

MARKET-CROSSES, crosses erected in market places, i.e. village centres

MARRY, indeed

MARS, the god of war

MATCH, 'cunning match', clever game

MEAN FOR POWERS, bargaining chip for obtaining soldiers

MEANS, 'base second means', mere secondary tools

MEDICINES, love-potions

MEET, wise

MEETING, meeting-place (III ii 174)

MELT, yield to your emotions

MEMENTO MORI, reminder of death

MERCURY, the messenger god, who was portrayed as having a winged cap and feet

MERE, utter (IV i 64)

MERLIN, ancient magician of King Arthur's court

METEOR, (i) atmospheric disturbance of any kind (believed to originate in the 'one substance' of earthly vapours) (I i 10); (ii) i.e. red pimples on Bardolph's face (II iv 310); (iii) meteor (V i 19)

METHINKS, it seems to me

METRE BALLAD-MONGERS, singers of doggerel ballads

METTLE, (i) spirit, valour (IV iii 22, V iv 24);

(ii) metal (which will not 'run', i.e. melt) (pun on (i) and (ii), II iv 338)

MICHAELMAS, 29 September

MICHER, truant (who neglects duty and goes blackberrying)

MILLINER, seller of perfumed gloves and other fancy goods

MINCING, affected

MINION, favourite

MISPRISION, misunderstanding

MISS, 'have a heavy miss of thee', (i) sadly miss you; (ii) miss your heavy body (pun, V iv 105)

MISTREADINGS, sins

MOE CORRIVALS, more allies of equal worth

MOIETY, share

MOLDWARP, mole

MOOR DITCH, open sewer in London

MORE AND LESS, men of greater and lesser rank

MORROW, morning

MOTIONS, expressions

MOUTHED, (i) gaping; (ii) speaking of bravery in battle (pun, I iii 97)

MOVING . . . WITH, including in

MUDDY, dull-witted

MUSTACHIO PURPLE-HU'D MALT-WORMS, long-mustached purple-faced drunkards

MUTUAL, united

NAUGHTY VARLET, wicked scoundrel

NEAT'S-TONGUE, ox-tongue

NECK, 'in the neck of', immediately after

NETHER, lower

NETHER-STOCKS, stockings

NEW-FALL'N RIGHT, right to your inheritance on your father's recent death

NEWGATE FASHION, chained two by two, like prisoners in Newgate Prison in London

NEWSMONGERS, scandal-mongers

NEXT, quickest (II i 8, III i 260); 'next of blood', heir to the throne

NICE, precarious

NICHOLAS', 'Saint Nicholas' clerks', highwaymen, robbers

NIGH, near

NONCE, occasion

NOTED, well-known

OB., obulus, or half-penny

O'ERRULED, guided

OFFICE, duty

OFFICER, officer of the law

OFF'RING SIDE, aggressors

OLD-FAC'D ANCIENT, tattered flag
OMNIPOTENT, complete and utter
ONEYERS, possibly (i) officials of the Exchequer (from a Latin phrase abbreviated 'o. ni.'); or (ii) comic colloquial word for 'ones'
OPINION, (i) arrogance (III i 185); (ii) public opinion (III ii 42); (iii) prestige (IV i 77); (iv) reputation (V iv 48)
OR . . . OR, either . . . or
ORB, 'obedient orb', orbit of obedience (as planets were believed to circle the earth in fixed spheres)
OSTLER, person in charge of horses at an inn
OTTER, subject of a traditional dispute as to whether it was a fish or a mammal
OUGHT, owed
OUT, 'out upon', away with, down with; 'out of fear', free of fear
OUT-FAC'D, frightened
OWE, possess (V ii 68)

PACES, 'hostile paces', battling cavalry
PAGAN, faithless
PAID, i.e. killed (II iv 184, 210, V iii 45, V iv 113)
PALISADOES, defences of iron-pointed stakes set in the ground
PANNIER, basket
PARAPETS, low defensive walls
PARAQUITO, parrot
PARCEL, part (III ii 159); 'parcel of a reckoning', details of a bill
PARLEY, (i) 'in such a parley', in the same language (i.e. tears) (III i 203); (ii) trumpet-call to a meeting to discuss the terms of a truce (IV iii 30 SD)
PARMACETI, spermaceti (medicinal ointment found in sperm whales)
PART, quality (V iv 118–19)
PARTICIPATION, 'vile participation', associating with the worthless
PARTIES SURE, persons involved are reliable
PARTLET, 'Dame Partlet', traditional name for a hen, and thus for a scolding woman
PASS THEM CURRENT, circulate them, have them accepted
PASSAGES, way
PASSION, pain (III i 35)
PATE, head
PATIENTLY, with patient fortitude
PAUL'S, St Paul's Cathedral in London
PAUSE UPON, postpone our decision about
PEACH, inform on you
PEAS AND BEANS, feed for horses

PEGASUS, mythological winged horse
PEPPERCORN, i.e. tiny and shrivelled
PEPPER'D, made it hot for (II iv 183); 'I have led my ragamuffins where they are pepper'd', i.e. deliberately, so as to be able to draw the dead soldiers' pay
PEPPER-GINGERBREAD, i.e. crumblingly feeble and barely spicy
PEREMPTORILY, positively
PERFECT, 'I am too perfect in', I understand only too well; 'perfect in lying down', proficient in lying down (with sexual suggestion)
PERSONAL, personally engaged
PHARAOH'S LEAN KINE, the lean cows of Pharaoh's dream in Genesis xli
PHOEBUS, the sun
PICK-PURSE, 'At hand, quoth pick-purse', ready, said the pickpocket (a popular saying)
PICK-THANKS, flatterers
PISMIRES, ants
PIZZLE, penis
PLACE, 'in place and in account', in your position and authority
PLAGUE (OF, ON), curse on
PLANTAGENET, Henry IV's family name
PLAY, 'play it off', drink it down; 'play the trumpet to', (i) act as herald to, announce; (ii) blow like a trumpet (pun, V i 4)
PLUM'D LIKE ESTRIDGES, wearing plumes like ostriches
POCKET-UP WRONG, (i) submit to wrongs; (ii) put the unpaid bills that wrong others in your pocket (pun, III iii 160)
POINTED AT, i.e. such an object of scorn and disapproval
POINTS, sword-points (but at II iv 208 Poins takes 'points' to mean the laces holding together doublet and hose)
POLICY, cunning, deceit
POLITICIAN, unprincipled schemer
POMGARNET, Pomegranate (the name of another room in the tavern)
PONTIFICAL, 'robe pontifical', bishop's or Pope's ceremonial robe
POOP, stern (usual location of flagship's lantern)
POPINJAY, parrot, flashily dressed chatterer
PORTEND, signify
PORTENT, omen
PORTLY, majestic, stately
POSSESS'D, informed (IV i 40)
POSSESSION, i.e. the possessor of the crown, Richard II
POST (n.), messenger

POSTED, rode in haste

POT OF ALE, mug of ale (suggesting Hal's taste for the low life of the taverns)

POULTER'S HARE, hare hung up for sale in a poultry shop

POUNCET-BOX, perfume box with perforated lid

POWDER (v.), salt

POWER, army

POX, venereal disease (thus the appropriateness of Hal's oath to 'my hostess')

PRECEDENT, example worth following

PREDICAMENT, (i) category; (ii) dangerous situation (pun, I iii 168)

PRESENCE, manner (I iii 17)

PRESENTLY, at once

PRESS (n.), power of military conscription; (v.), draft as soldiers

PRICK, 'pricks me on', spurs me on; 'prick me off', (i) chooses me for death (as items on a list were pricked, or checked, off); (ii) puts a hole in me (pun, V i 130)

PRIDE, height (I i 60)

PRITHEE, pay thee, I pray thee

PRODIGALS, i.e. Prodigal Sons (the son in the parable in Luke xv 11–32 is so hungry that he envies the pigs their husks)

PRODIGY, omen

PROFESS NOT, do not claim as my profession

PROFESSION, i.e. robbery

PROFITED, proficient

PROGRESS, royal journey

PROOF, trial (II ii 66, V ii 55)

PROPORTION, 'in the first proportion', of the greatest size

PROSPEROUS HOPE, hopes of success

PROVISO, 'But with proviso and exception', except according to his condition

PRUNE (v.), preen (like a falcon)

PUDDING, stuffing

PUKE-STOCKING, dark woollen stocking

PUNY, inexperienced, apprentice

PUPIL-AGE, youth (i.e. it has just struck twelve)

PURCHASE, (i) stolen loot (II i 85); (ii) value (III iii 38)

PURGE, (i) acquit (III ii 20); (ii) repent; (iii) take laxatives (pun on (ii) and (iii), V iv 162)

QUALITY, party (IV iii 36)

QUESTION, doubt (IV i 68)

QUICK-CONCEIVING DISCONTENTS, minds which are quick to understand because discontented

QUIDDITIES, quibbles; 'in the quips and thy quiddities', in a mood for wit

QUILT, soldier's quilted jacket (which was also called a 'jack' – thus Hal puns on Falstaff's name)

QUIT, acquit myself of

RABBIT-SUCKER, baby rabbit (hung up for sale)

RACKS, instruments of torture on which the victim was slowly stretched

RAILING, scolding

RAMPING, rearing up

RASH, quick (to burn up)

RATED, (i) scolded (I ii 81, IV iii 99); (ii) 'rated sinew', mainstay they had counted on (IV iv 17)

RAZES, roots

READ TO, taught anything to

REAP'D, 'chin new reap'd', beard newly trimmed

REASONS, (i) reasons; (ii) raisins (pun, II iv 231)

REBUKE, violent check

RECEIPT OF FERN-SEED, recipe for fern-seed (which was supposed to make one invisible)

RECKONING (n.), bill, settlement of an account; 'call'd her to a reckoning', asked for the bill (with sexual suggestion)

REDBREAST TEACHER, teacher of singing to robins

REDEEMING TIME, making amends for wasted time (Hal's words echo Ephesians v 16)

REMEMBER, remind (V i 32)

REMOV'D, not closely involved in the plot (IV i 35)

RENDEZVOUS, refuge

REPRISAL, prize

REPROOF, disproof (I ii 183, III ii 23); 'in reproof of many tales devis'd', having disproved many false accusations

REPUTELESS, unknown

RESOLUTION, courage (in thievery)

RESPECT, attention (IV iii 31); 'in respect of', on account of

RETIREMENT, (i) 'comfort of retirement', support on which to fall back (IV i 56); (ii) retreat (V iv 6)

REVERSION, inheritance still to be received, i.e. hope of future support

REVOLT (n.), treason

REVOLTED, runaway (IV ii 25)

REWARD, 'follow, as they say, for reward', i.e. like hounds that have brought down a deer, for the reward of scraps of its flesh

RIBS, i.e. fat man (II iv 106)

RIDGE, crossbar of the gallows

RIGHT, 'divide our right According to our threefold order ta'en', divide up what is ours by right according to our three-part arrangement

RIVO, a drinking cry

ROB, i.e. rob the tavernkeeper by running away from him (II iv 66)

ROUNDLY, frankly, plainly

ROYAL, (i) of the royal family; (ii) a ten-shilling coin (puns, I ii 135, II iv 280 – with further pun on 'noble', a coin worth six shillings and eightpence)

RUB THE ELBOW, show great pleasure

RUDE, uncivilised and violent

RUFFIAN, devil (a morality-play character)

RUNS ME UP WITH LIKE ADVANTAGE, flows across my land, cutting off just as much

SACK, Spanish white wine (sweet)

SALAMANDER, i.e. in Bardolph's face (salamanders were supposed to live in fire)

SALLIES AND RETIRES, attacks and retreats

SALPETRE, an ingredient in gunpowder

SALVATION, 'take it already upon their salvation', swear by the salvation of their souls

SANGUINE, red-faced (and thus apparently valorous)

SARCENET, thin silk, i.e. flimsy

SAVING YOUR REVERENCE, i.e. pardon my language

'SBLOOD, by God's blood (an oath)

SCAPE, escape

SCEPTRE, staff emblematic of monarchy

SCOPE, 'natural scope', normal freedom of words

SCORE, put on the bill

SCORING, (i) running up a bill; (ii) cutting (pun, V iii 31)

SCOT, (i) Scotsman; (ii) a small payment (puns, I iii 214–15); 'scot and lot', in full (these were the names of parish taxes)

SCOURGE OF GREATNESS, power as king to punish

SCUTCHEON, shield painted with coat of arms for display at a funeral

SEAL-RING, ring used for sealing letters and documents

SEAT, (i) dwelling (I i 65); (ii) estates (V i 45)

SECURE, safely

SEDGY, reed-covered

SEEMING MERCY, semblance of mercy

SEMBLABLY FURNISH'D, appearing in dress and arms

SENSIBLE OF, capable of feeling

SERVE, i.e. of your apprenticeship (which ordinarily lasted seven years) (II iv 38)

SERVICES, 'bought out their services', paid to be released from military service

SET, seated (II iv 423); 'set a match', planned a robbery; 'set the exact wealth of our states', stake the entire value of our estates; 'set off his head', not taken into account against him; 'set to a leg', set a broken leg

SETTER, one who plans a robbery

SEVEN STARS, the Pleiades

SEVERALLY, separately

SHADE, darkness

SHADOW, (i) 'shadow of succession', frivolous and unsubstantial heir-apparent (III ii 99); (ii) likeness (V iv 30)

SHAPE OF LIKELIHOOD, probability, the most likely course of events

SHARING, dividing up the loot

SHAV'D, (i) shaved; (ii) cheated; (iii) a victim of syphilis (causing baldness) (pun, III iii 58)

SHELTER, hide

SHORT-WINDED ACCENTS, breathless words

SHOT-FREE, (i) without paying the bill; (ii) unwounded by cannon-shot (pun, V iii 30)

SHOTTEN HERRING, a herring that has deposited its roe (and is therefore very thin)

SHUFFLING, hobbled

SICK, despised (IV iii 57)

SINCERITY, 'very sincerity of fear', pure fear

SIRRAH, term of address generally used only to inferiors, implying great familiarity

SKIMBLE-SKAMBLE STUFF, nonsense

SKIPPING, frivolous

SMOOTH, comforting (I i 66)

SMUG, smooth

SNEAK-CUP, one who steals his drink

SNORTING, snoring

SNUFF, 'Took it in snuff', (i) inhaled it; (ii) took offence at it (pun, I iii 41)

SOFT, wait a minute, hold on

SOLUS, alone

SOOTH, 'in (good) sooth', truly

SOOTHERS, flatterers

SOUS'D GURNET, pickled fish

SOVEREIGN TRUST, (i) a command fit for a

108

prince; (ii) the trust of the King (pun, III ii 161)

SOVEREIGNEST, finest

SPANISH-POUCH, wallet of Spanish leather

SPEAK, i.e. cry 'Hands up' (II i 74)

SPEAR-GRASS, variety of rough-edged grass

SPEED, 'be your speed', bring you success

SPHERE, orbit

SPIRIT, evil spirit (II iv 357)

SPITE, 'deadly spite', vexing circumstance

SPLEEN, fiery impetuosity, rashness (of which the weasel was believed to have a great deal)

SPRING, source (V ii 23)

SQUIER, square, measuring rule

SQUIRES OF THE NIGHT'S BODY, attendants on the night (with puns on 'knight' and 'bawdy', I ii 23)

STAFF, 'my staff of office did I break', i.e. he deserted his post as Richard II's Steward of the Household

STAIN'D, blood-stained (V iv 13)

STAMP, 'of this season's stamp', of this age

STAND, 'Stand', robber's cry to his victim; 'stands to his word', keeps his word; 'stand for', (i) fight for, in a robbery; (ii) be worth (punning on 'royal', a ten-shilling coin) (pun, I ii 135–6); 'Stand close', hide; 'stand the push', tolerate the impudence; 'stand to it', take a stand; 'stand full fairly for the day', seem on the way to victory

STANDING TUCK, rapier on legs

STARK, rigid

START (n.), 'start of spleen', fit of bad temper; (v.), 'start away', wander from the point

STARTING-HOLE, refuge for a hunted animal, hiding place

STARVE, (i) grow numb with cold (II i 25); (ii) die (II ii 18)

STATE, (i) chair of state, throne (II iv 366, 368); (ii) formal public appearances (III ii 57); (iii) dignity (III ii 62)

STAY, await, wait

STEPS ME, steps

STEWED PRUNE, slang for 'prostitute'

STILL, continually, always

STOCK-FISH, dried cod

STOMACH, appetite

STORE, 'your store', all your wealth

STOUT, valiant

STRAIGHT, immediately

STRAIN TOO FAR, exaggerate

STRAIT, strict

STRANDS, lands

STRAPPADO, torture in which the victim was strung up by the arms and then dropped suddenly

STRIKE, assault, rob (II i 73, II ii 80)

STRUCK FOWL, wounded bird

STUDIES (n.), interests

SUBMISSION, admission of guilt

SUBORNATION, 'murderous subornation', secretly bringing about a murder

SUBTLE, crafty

SUDDENLY, very soon

SUE HIS LIVERY, sue for his inheritance (which had been seized by the crown)

SUFFER, permit

SUFFERANCES, sufferings

SUGAR, sometimes used for sweetening wine (most frequently by the elderly, which is the point of Poins' gibe at I ii 109)

SUGAR-CANDY, given to fighting-cocks to ward off breathlessness

SUGGESTION, incitement

SUITS, (i) petitions to the king, preferment (I ii 69); (ii) clothing of executed convicts, which went to the hangman (I ii 70)

SULLEN GROUND, dull background

SUN IN MARCH, believed to cause fevers by drawing unhealthy vapours from the earth

SUPERFLUOUS TO, concerned with irrelevancies as to

SUPPLY, 'looks he not for supply?', does he not expect reinforcements?

SUPPOSITION . . . SHALL BE STUCK FULL OF EYES, suspicion will mean that we are being watched

SURE, 'make him sure', i.e. make sure he's dead

SURFEITED WITH, grew tired of

SURPRIS'D, captured

SURVEY, 'takes survey of', oversees

SUTTON CO'FIL', Sutton Coldfield, about 20 miles north-west of Coventry

SWALLOWING, being swallowed

SWORD-AND-BUCKLER, inferior ruffian (sword and buckler, or small shield, were the arms of the lower classes)

SYMPATHIZE, agree in mood

TAFFETA, 'flame-coloured taffeta', traditional dress of prostitutes

TAILOR, profession known for singing

TAKE, 'rightly taken', (i) correctly understood; (ii) justly arrested (pun, II iv 316); 'take me with you', make yourself clear to me

TALL, valiant

TALLOW, i.e. fat man

TALLOW-CATCH, pan to catch drippings under roasted meat

TARGET, shield

TASK, 'task me to', test; 'task'd', taxed

TASKING, 'How show'd his tasking?', how did he present the challenge?

TASTE, try out (IV i 119)

TAVERN, (i) tavern; (ii) tabern, a tabor or non-military drum (pun, III iii 205)

TEDIOUS, laborious (III i 48)

TEEMING, fruitful, over-full

TEMPER, character (III i 170)

TEMPLE HALL, hall of the Inner Temple in London, a popular meeting-place

TEMPTED, provoked

TENCH, fish whose red spots make it appear flea-bitten

TENDER, 'mak'st some tender of', have some regard for

TENOUR, significance (IV iv 7); 'misuse the tenour of thy kinsman's trust', abuse the essence of the trust placed in you by your kinsman, Hotspur

TERMAGANT, violent

THICK-EY'D, dim-sighted

THIEVES OF THE DAY'S BEAUTY, wasters of daylight, idlers (with pun on 'booty', I ii 23–4)

THIS DAY MORNING, this morning

THOUGHT, 'with a thought', in a flash

THREE FINGERS, i.e. three fingers of fat (a finger was ¾ of an inch)

THRILL, run cold

THRIVE, succeed

TICKLE YE FOR, entertain you with my imitation of

TICKLE-BRAIN, (i) dim-wit; (ii) kind of strong liquor (pun, II iv 386)

TILT WITH LIPS, i.e. kiss

TIME, (i) lifetime (III ii 36, 151); (ii) the times (IV i 25)

TINKER, profession known for heavy drinking and for speaking in a special slang

TITAN, the sun (red-faced Falstaff at his sack is like the sun shining on butter)

TITHE, tenth part

TOASTS-AND-BUTTER, cowards

TOSS, 'toss'd with', troubled with; 'good enough to toss', good enough to be tossed on the enemies' pikes

TOWN'S END, the town gates (where beggars generally congregated)

TRACE, follow

TRADE-FALL'N, out of work

TRAIN (n.), retinue; (v.), lure (V ii 21)

TRANQUILLITY, i.e. those who don't have to work for a living

TRANSFORMATION, mutilation

TREAD UPON, i.e. treat with contempt

TRENCH HIM, make the river run

TRENCHING, (i) wounding; (ii) cutting trenches in battlefields

TRICK, characteristic (II iv 391, V ii 11)

TRIM (adj.), 'trim reckoning', fine account; (n.), 'in their trim', i.e. decked out like victims ready for sacrifice

TRIMMED UP, adorned

TRISTFUL, sorrowful

TRIUMPH (n.), torchlight procession

TROTH, truth; 'by my troth', truly, indeed

TROYANS, good fellows, boon companions

TRUE MAN, honest man

TRUNCHEON, club, cudgel

TRUNK OF HUMOURS, container of disease-causing bodily fluids

TUN, (i) barrel; (ii) ton (pun, II iv 432)

TURK GREGORY, an imaginary ruthless tyrant (Turks were proverbial types of pagan ferocity: Gregory suggests Popes Gregory VII and Gregory XIII, both of whom were known for inciting acts of violence)

TURN, 'turn head against', (i) turns toward, faces; (ii) leads an army against (pun, III ii 102); 'turn our offers contrary', misrepresent our offers

UNBORN, future

UNCERTAIN, unreliable (II iii 9–10)

UNDER-SKINKER, under-tapster, assistant waiter

UNEVEN, troubling (I i 50)

UNGRACIOUS, graceless, profane

UNJOINTED, rambling

UNJUST, dishonest

UNMINDED, unnoticed

UNPROVIDED, unprepared

UNSORTED, unfavourable

UNTHOUGHT-OF, unheard-of, despised

UNWASH'D, 'with unwash'd hands', without delay

UNYOKED HUMOUR, unrestrained inclination (*unrestrained caprice*)

UP, in arms (III ii 120)

USAGE, treatment

USE, (i) try (III i 176); (ii) show (III ii 83); (iii) treat (V i 59, 61)

UTTERED, 'out of anger can be uttered', can be angrily described in public

VALUED, 'Our business valued', considering the things we have to do

VANITY, (i) worldliness (I ii 79, II iv 438); (ii) frivolity (V iii 33, V iv 106); (iii) empty boast (V iv 74); 'vanity in years', ageing embodiment of worldliness (Vanity was a morality-play character)

VARLET, scoundrel

VASSAL, slavish

VASTY DEEP, abyss of the lower world

VAUNTING, boasting

VELVET-GUARDS, i.e. middle-class citizens dressed in their Sunday clothes with velvet trimmings

VERIEST VARLET, most complete scoundrel

VICE, like 'iniquity', 'ruffian', and 'vanity', a character who corrupted virtue in the morality plays (but these characters were usually portrayed as being much younger than Falstaff)

VIGILANT, wakeful

VINTNER, tavernkeeper

VIZARDS, masks

VOCATION, calling (Falstaff ridicules this Puritan notion; see I Corinthians vii 20)

VOUCHSAFE, grant

WAIT ON US, are at our command

WAND'RING, 'that wand'ring knight so fair', apparently a line from a ballad on the Knight of the Sun, a hero of Spanish romances

WANT, lack

WANTON, (i) luxurious (III i 213); (ii) exuberant (IV i 103); (iii) unruly (V i 50)

WANTONNESS, frivolous behaviour

WARD, defensive stance in fencing (I ii 181, II iv 186)

WARRANT, assure

WATCH (n.), band of officers of the law; (v.), (i) lie awake (II iii 44); (ii) revel, carouse; (iii) keep vigil (pun on (ii) and (iii), and reference to Matthew xxvi 41, II iv 266)

WATER-COLOURS, i.e. thin pretexts

WATERING, 'breathe in your watering', pause for breath in your drinking

WEAVER, frequently the profession of psalm-singing Puritans

WELL-BESEEMING, handsome, fitting

WELL-RESPECTED, well-considered

WELL SAID, well done (V iv 75)

WELSH, 'speaks better Welsh', (i) brags better; (ii) speaks finer gibberish (pun, III i 50); 'Welsh hook', a weapon which has no 'cross' (i.e. cross-shaped hilt) on which to swear

WHELP, offspring

WHERE TO HAVE HER, what to make of her (with sexual suggestion)

WHEREABOUT, why

WHEREUPON, on what grounds

WHILE, 'God help the while', God help these times

WHIT, bit

WHOLE, settled (IV i 25)

WHORESON, miserable, wretched; 'whoreson caterpillars', wretched parasites

WILD OF KENT, Weald of Kent (once-forested area of the county)

WILDFIRE, 'ball of wildfire', firework

WILFUL-BLAME, blamable for wilfulness

WIND (n.), 'Is the wind in that door?', is that the way things are going? (v.), wheel about (IV i 109)

WINDMILL, i.e. very noisy and cold place

WISDOM, 'for wisdom cries out in the streets, and no man regards it', Hal's paraphrase of Proverbs i 20–24

WITCH, bewitch

WITHAL, (i) with (II iv 499, III ii 15, 21, V ii 95); (ii) in addition (III i 143, IV iii 103)

WORSHIP, honour

WRONGS IN US, injuries done by us

WRUNG IN THE WITHERS, rubbed raw across the shoulders

YARD, yardstick

YEDWARD, dialectal variant of Edward

YOUNGER, earlier (V i 71); 'younger sons of younger brothers', i.e. men with no hope of an inheritance

YOUNKER, greenhorn, easy mark (from the 'younger', the Prodigal Son, who was portrayed frequently as having lost his money to loose women)

ZEAL, emotion, affection

ZOUNDS, by God's wounds (an oath)